THE PEOPLE'S REPUBLIC OF THE DISAPPEARED

Stories from inside China's system for enforced disappearances

Edited by Michael Caster

Foreword by Teng Biao

For more victim stories, profiles, news and materials related to China's system for enforced disappearances, visit:

RSDLmonitor.com

ISBN: 978-0-9993706-0-5

First edition.

Keywords: Enforced disappearance, China, Human Rights, Criminal Justice, International law

Also available as Kindle book:

ISBN: 978-0-9993706-1-2

https://SafeguardDefenders.com

REVIEWS

A "noteworthy" and "deserving" book.
- **Jerome A. Cohen, Professor at New York University (School of Law)**

...the most comprehensive collective portrait to date, *Disappeared* compiles powerful first-person accounts.
- **Terence Halliday, Co-Director of Center on Law and Globalization, American Bar Foundation**

...eye-opening and courageous. ...help you better understand the Middle Kingdom.
- **June Cheng, WORLD magazine**

...a very heavy [reading] session.
- **Kate Whitehead, South China Morning Post**

The narrators tell of physical and psychological abuse, beatings and sleep deprivation, humiliations, isolation... rare in their detail.
- **Steven Lee Meyer, the New York Times**

Direct and compelling. A rare and important collection.
- **Eva Pils, Reader in Transnational Law, King's College London**

...this book is a necessary eye opener. ...will add depth and clarity.
- **Yaxue Cao, Director of ChinaChange.org**

...a profoundly important book. If you want to understand China beneath the dollar signs and infrastructure projects, read this book.
- **Benedict Rogers, Deputy Chair of [UK] Conservative Party Human Rights Committee, founder of Hong Kong Watch**

...essential reading for academics and journalists, governments and nonprofit workers. ...worthwhile reading for anyone studying authoritarian regimes and the struggle for human rights.
- **Magnus Fiskesjö, Professor at Cornell University**

...reading this is like taking a direct glimpse at the cruelty and brutality that are the heart of Communist Party rule.
- **Kong Tsung-gan, Medium, The Best Human Rights Books of 2017**

Dedicated to **Wang Quanzhang**

Wang Quanzhang, lawyer - father - husband, disappeared on 3 August 2015. Family, friends, and his lawyers have neither seen nor heard from him since he was taken and not long after placed under Residential Surveillance at a Designated Location (RSDL), China's system for enforced disappearances.

Credible sources have claimed that Wang has been subjected to electro-shock torture, and at the time of writing, more than two years since his disappearance, his case remains unresolved. He has not even been given a trial. Police have also subjected his wife and young son to nearly ceaseless harassment and intimidation.

Wang's refusal to disavow his beliefs, his refusal to be paraded on Chinese state television to "confess," or to incriminate his friends, coworkers, and other lawyers, have made him the government's prime target in its "war on lawyers" campaign, also called the "709 Crackdown," after the date (9 July 2015) when it all began.

His courage and devotion to human rights in the face of great adversity should be an inspiration to all.

ACKNOWLEDGEMENTS

We would like to extend a heartfelt thank you to everyone who supported this project.

Most importantly, this book couldn't have happened without all the brave people who came forward to share their stories. In China, merely to speak of your experiences in Residential Surveillance at a Designated Location (RSDL) can itself pose a threat, and many who have chosen to speak out have been detained again after speaking with the media, foreign organizations or researchers.

Those who have shared their stories in this book have done so at considerable risk to themselves, but they have done so because they agree that there is a real need to expose China's systematic use of Enforced Disappearances, and to help future victims of RSDL to be better prepared for what awaits them. We hope their stories lead to greater awareness and inspire action against this abusive system.

Many others have wanted to share their stories, but either felt it was too hard to revisit their painful experiences or that the threat of reprisal was too strong to allow their stories to be published, for now. Others have offered their time to be interviewed, so that we can more accurately present RSDL, or given their feedback on draft versions. To all those who volunteered their time, their knowledge, and their experiences for this book, we would like to offer our heartfelt thanks. We would like to especially thank Zhang Zhiming for all his translation support. Dinah Gardner also deserves a big thank you for her help during the frantic final stages.

TABLE OF CONTENTS

Foreword | **TENG BIAO**

Atrocity in the name of the law

Those holding unchecked power often seek to hide their cruelty behind euphemisms. In China, classic examples range from "land reform" to the "Cultural Revolution." You can't easily see the cruelty from the surface of such words. Expressions like "the three year natural disaster," used by the Communist Party to describe the Great Leap Forward of 1958 to 1961 in which tens of millions died, or the "6/4 counterrevolutionary riot," the description of the Tiananmen Democracy movement, are shameless acts of misrepresenting history and reversing right and wrong. Do "Legal Education Centers" really have anything to do with law or education? No. They are Black Jails for arbitrarily detaining and tormenting politically sensitive groups around the country.

"Residential Surveillance at a Designated Location" (RSDL) is the latest euphemism.

Tyranny is not only reflected in murder, evil laws, and crackdowns; it is reflected even more in the minor details. This book is a collection of details, vividly reflecting China's cruelty.

Much remains unknown about RSDL, and for that reason this book is an invaluable look into the rarely exposed systematic tyranny behind the euphemism of "Residential Surveillance at a Designated Location."

Looking into its legislative history, RSDL was first envisioned in the 1997 Criminal Procedure Law (CPL), which dictated a special form of Residential Surveillance to be applied to those suspects without a fixed residence. However, with police having near unlimited powers, it is little wonder that the regulation has been used for repression.

The most famous democracy advocate in China, the deceased Nobel Peace Prize laureate, Liu Xiaobo, was placed under Residential Surveillance after he was taken in December 2008. His crime had been signing "Charter 08," a petition calling for democracy and political liberalization in China. Obviously, Liu Xiaobo did not belong to the category of "suspects without fixed residence" and should have been allowed to serve his Residential Surveillance with his family at his home. His lawyer should have been allowed to visit him anytime. Instead, Liu was effectively disappeared during his seven months of Residential Surveillance, before being sentenced in a mockery of a trial to 11 years in prison for inciting subversion of state power. On 13 July 2017, Liu Xiaobo died of liver cancer, likely treatable had he not been a prisoner of the state. His wife, Liu Xia, has also been disappeared at times, denied contact with the outside world with no legal basis or justification.

During the 2011 "Jasmine Revolution," [1] the authorities kidnapped and secretly detained human rights defenders on a large scale, in a gangland act of criminality under the banner of "National Security." Human rights lawyer Liu Shihui (Chapter 2) reflected on his secret detention. "I was beaten so badly that I needed stitches. My ribs were in extreme pain, which continued to interrupt my sleep for days. I wished that I would be transferred to a detention center."[2]

Similarly, [activist] Tang Jingling was not allowed to sleep for upwards of ten days. In the end, he felt "trembling, numbness of hands, and a bad feeling in his heart, that his life was in great danger, and only then did the police just allow him to sleep one or two hours a day."[3]

Writer Ye Du was held in a Guangzhou Police Training Center for 96 days, like lawyer Sui Muqing (Chapter 10). Ye recalled, "[I] didn't see sunlight for over a month. I was subjected to 22 hours of interrogation every day. I was given one hour for eating, one hour for sleeping, until the 7th day when my stomach had massive bleeding."[4]

Hua Ze's book, *In the Shadow of the Rising Dragon*, published in 2013, records the experiences of 47 activists caught up during the Jasmine Revolution. I was one of them.

After I was kidnapped, I was detained in secret for 70 days. I was told that I was being placed under Residential Surveillance. No one ever told me their name, department, or position. Nobody ever showed me a work permit, search warrant, or any legal documents. I suffered. During this time, I was beaten, deprived of sleep, forced to maintain stress positions, forced to wear handcuffs for 24 hours a day for 36 days, threatened, abused, forced to write a confession, and otherwise ill-treated. Even now, years later, it is hard to put it into words.

RSDL is classified as a non-custodial coercive measure, but in reality it has not only became a system for prolonged, pre-trial detention outside a formal, legal location, but has also become a more severe, more terrible, coercive measure than normal criminal detention. RSDL is not limited by detention center regulations, nor any real supervision at all. The chances of torture are greatly increased; in fact, torture has become rampant under RSDL.

The authorities must find RSDL to be a very convenient and effective way for dealing with rights defenders, judging by its indiscriminate use since the CPL was revised in 2012.

Article 73 of the CPL, stipulates that, "Residential Surveillance shall be enforced in the residence of the suspect or defendant. For those without a fixed residence, it may be enforced in a designated location. When... enforcement in the residence might impede the investigation, it may also be enforced in a designated location upon the approval of the People's Procuratorate or Public Security organ at the level above."

The police can decide for themselves if someone is to be placed in RSDL, which means the police decide who is to be disappeared.

It is little wonder that this was one of the most controversial articles during legislative reform, leading many commentators, myself included, to call it the "Jasmine Article." This is because it appeared to legalize enforced disappearances, which had become more common during the Jasmine Revolution crackdown.

The CPL stipulates that RSDL "must not be enforced in a detention center or special case-handling area;" but in reality, all RSDL is enforced at special case-handling areas run by the Public or State Security Bureaus, or it is carried out at euphemistically named "training centers," "prevention bases," "anti-corruption education bases," or sometimes even hotels that have been specially converted into secret detention facilities known as Black Jails.

The law permits for exceptions where family members don't even need to be informed, and allows the state to deny access to a lawyer. These exceptions, which have now become the norm, have turned RSDL into a de facto enforced disappearance, exactly what the RSDL system seeks to achieve.

During suppression of the "Jasmine Revolution" in 2011 and the "709 Crackdown" starting in 2015, [5] terrifying enforced disappearances became common experiences within the human rights community. The most serious example is lawyer Wang Quanzhang. While I am writing this, Wang's fate and whereabouts have remained uncertain for over two years. The cruelty and brutality of RSDL is clearly visible for the world to see.

In 2010, the Chinese government refused to sign the International Convention for the Protection of All Persons from Enforced Disappearance. This was an irresponsible act but far from surprising. Enforced disappearances are nothing new in China. High-profile examples include the 17 May 1995 disappearance of the then six-year-old Panchen Lama, who had been confirmed by the Dalai Lama, and the widespread disappearance of Uyghurs following the July 2009 Urumqi riots. Still, the legalization of enforced disappearances in the CPL is shameful.

According to the original intention of the law, Residential Surveillance should only be a monitoring location. It is not to be used for interrogation or custodial purposes. However, the facilities used for

RSDL have not only become specialized interrogation facilities, they have become even harsher than prisons and detention centers.

These custom-built prisons, spread across China, which are not allowed to be called prisons, have become terrifying torture centers where all manner of abuse is common: long periods of sleep deprivation, beatings, electrocution, forcibly handcuffed and shackled, confined to tiger stools and dangling chairs for long and painful periods, subjected to fumigation of the eyes by smoke, subjected to stress positions, denial of food and water, denied hygiene, extensive and continuous interrogation sessions, threats of violence, or threats to family. Everyone placed in RSDL is kept in solitary confinement.

Torture during many disappearances is well documented in a number of high profile cases. The accounts have sometimes been too much for people to bear reading about. Many rights defenders related to the 709 Crackdown, such as Li Heping, Li Chunfu, Xie Yanyi, Li Shuyun, and Gou Hongguo, have explained how they were forcibly fed unidentified medicine, leading to different painful symptoms.

Families of some of the 709 lawyers published an open letter in which they wrote, "Lawyer Li Chunfu, Xie Yanyi, Xie Yang, and Li Heping were all tortured to such a degree that they became different people from who they were before they were taken, some only 40 years old but looking more than 60."[6]

Until now, most of what we know about RSDL has come from scattered reports or open letters from family members. This book is the first to present a fuller picture of the suffering imposed under RSDL.

Jiang Xiaoyu, an IT worker, writes in Chapter 8 of being told:

I can make you disappear for years. Even your wife and daughter won't know where you are.

Another victim, lawyer Chen Zhixiu, details in Chapter 4:

It wasn't until the third day that they gave me two small steamed buns and a few green vegetables. The size of the two buns together was still smaller than the palm of my hand. I felt that I was going to lose consciousness. I felt dizzy all the time because of lack of food and sleep, but I was still expected to submit to being interrogated. If I started to wobble in the chair they would make horrifying sounds to snap me awake.

I myself had experiences such as these during my detention. I tried to distract myself with memories, talked to myself, outlined literature and found other ways to keep from going crazy, since I was deprived of all forms of communication. Once I accidently saw a Party newspaper. I was very excited. Finally, I could read some text! When they played a propaganda film to brainwash me, I was happy just to hear the background music.

It doesn't matter if it is physical or mental torture. Both are hard to describe and express in words. However, the most painful thing is not the torture itself. For prisoners of conscience held in secret, I have found, there are two things that lead to even greater suffering:

One is being subjected to forced confession. Several individuals in this book describe with previously undisclosed details the experiences of delivering a forced confession. Those who have stepped onto the road of human rights defense face enormous pressure, living with threats to their family and heavy prison sentences. Many have been forced to confess. The authorities have used these confession videos to broadcast propaganda on state television, to confuse public opinion, to crack down on the will of resistance and dehumanize those who resist, and to turn rights defender against rights defender. It is used to split supporters. This may be the hardest part for China's many political prisoners.

The authorities don't always achieve their purpose but they more or less always have an impact. Many people have suffered the pain of misunderstanding and have grown distant from others. Many have quit rights defense because they were ashamed of themselves.

Secondly, those detained in secret have almost all experienced the indescribable suffering of having their families threatened or persecuted. In general, those who have chosen to become rights defenders under this kind of dictatorship are already aware of the risks and are prepared. When we are "invited for tea" [a euphemism used to describe a police summons], placed under house arrest, detained or tortured, nothing can stop our fighting spirit. But for the authorities to achieve the greatest deterrence, all they need to do is apply the threat of pain to our family members. This has become a common tactic used by the authorities, and used with growing expertise. As with my own experience, the hardest thing for activists fighting for freedom is how to balance conflict between family and social responsibilities.

People compromise, yield, fall silent, or give up after their family has been threatened or attacked. The Chinese Communist Party understands this clearly. I have written about the Party's assault against the family members of rights defenders before.

RSDL goes far beyond normal detention. Serious human rights violations are widespread. It goes against the rule of law. It should be abolished. But under the One Party Dictatorship, the lack of judicial independence or freedom of expression, the state has instead expanded its suppression of the human rights movement and hurriedly broadened the use of RSDL in the name of "stability maintenance."

The publication of this book has great importance and meaning: to reveal the truth, record the misery, and provide evidence of guilt. It is an indispensable signpost on the road to justice.

Dr Teng Biao is a human rights lawyer, formerly a lecturer at the China University of Politics and Law, and currently a visiting scholar at the US-Asia Law Institute, New York University. He co-founded two human rights NGOs in Beijing—the Open Constitution Initiative and China Against the Death Penalty, in 2003 and 2010 respectively. Because of his human rights work, he was abducted and detained by Chinese secret police in 2008 and 2011.

Introduction | MICHAEL CASTER

The People's Republic of the Disappeared

It was early in January 2016. I woke up to find several frantic Telegram notifications. Checking my encrypted email, the three messages at the top of my inbox, each with a more troublesome subject line, grew to confirm what several of us had been fearing for days: the disappearances had reached our network.

I was in northern England, so that by the time I received the messages, several hours had already passed since they had been sent from Beijing. The last email, from a trusted human rights defender, confirmed that my colleague, Swedish citizen Peter Dahlin (Chapter 5), and his Chinese girlfriend Pan Jinling (Chapter 6) had been disappeared. In 2009, Peter and I, along with lawyer Wang Quanzhang, had co-founded the Chinese Urgent Action Working Group, or China Action, a Beijing-based human rights organization. Over the years, we had provided legal training for hundreds of barefoot lawyers[1] around China, operated legal aid stations to provide pro bono support for victims of government abuse, and produced a number of manuals on rights defense. Nothing contentious surely, except in China where protecting citizens' rights is treated as an assault on state supremacy. Peter was a foreseeable target within China's authoritarian state logic, and we had been preparing for the worst. That they would extend the attack to include Jinling, his girlfriend, who had nothing to do with the human rights community, was however a surprise, and the epitome of arbitrariness. An increasingly widespread practice, as Teng Biao mentions in the Foreword to this book, is the punishment of partners, parents, children, and siblings for the supposed crimes of their human rights defender family members.

Over the next week, more people from our organization would be *taken,* a euphemism for disappearance and arbitrary detention, where someone is denied contact with family, lawyers, diplomats, or foreign media. The world is left guessing whether they are alive or dead. The rights defender who had emailed me also said that he himself was preparing to be taken and asked me to help his family get out of China if he disappeared. Just as he feared, he too was later seized.

A few days after they disappeared, while I was still trying to work behind the scenes with the diplomatic community, believing quiet diplomatic pressure was the best strategy, Jinling recounts her first few days inside Residential Surveillance at a Designated Location (RSDL):

> *I realized they were going to leave me there, strapped into the wooden chair all night. After some time, I was feeling exhausted but no sooner had I closed my eyes than the guard screamed into my face. I was shocked... Again I felt myself nodding, but as soon as my eyes were barely closed the guard was right there in my face screaming. This was how I passed the night, deprived of sleep. It was horrible.*

Over the following weeks, I continued to focus my attention on coordinating international advocacy, from working behind the scenes with representatives of foreign governments, friends in the international human rights community, and later speaking publicly with foreign correspondents. I was growing frustrated by what seemed like a slow diplomatic response. Journalists did their best but also made mistakes. What was becoming apparent was that although by January 2016 many rights defenders had been disappeared across China under a criminal procedure that had existed since 2013, few people fully grasped the extent of RSDL.

Of course, RSDL hadn't come about without concerns from the human rights community; lawyers Teng Biao and Tang Jitian (Chapter 1) among others had been outspoken critics. On his personal blog in February 2012, then Chinese University of Hong Kong legal scholar, Joshua Rosenzweig, echoed such concerns when he commented that the authorities' habit of "operating in the blank spaces of the law and the hidden spaces of internal police regulations" would become entrenched if the then draft Criminal Procedure Law (CPL) went forward with its inclusion of RSDL.[2] Writing in the *New York Times,* also in February 2012, then Human Rights Watch China Researcher Nicholas Bequelin warned that under the guise of regulation, RSDL would "effectively legalize secret detentions and 'disappearances' of people viewed as political risks by the government."[3] Still, it has taken a long time for people to realize the severity of RSDL. As sociologists Sida Liu and Terence Halliday recall in *Criminal Defense in China,* in 2012 while some activists reacted with alarm at the possible legalization of a cruel practice, a number of other Chinese lawyers and scholars dismissed the risks of RSDL, believing it would be used with caution.[4]

Even through 2015 to 2016, as hundreds of rights defenders were disappearing for varying periods of time, observers and family members at first often responded with mild relief at hearing that their colleagues and loved ones had been placed under RSDL. Many still believed RSDL would amount to being softer than criminal detention and, some might say naively, that because it was a formal criminal procedure it would be less secretive and open to abuse than had been the extralegal system of Black Jails into which so many petitioners and human rights defenders had been disappeared over the previous decade.[5] They couldn't have been more wrong.

After Sui Muqing (Chapter 10) was first transferred to RSDL, some expressed relief. When Gou Hongguo's wife was alerted that he had been placed under RSDL, she recounted feeling "ecstatic," and only started to feel otherwise after having contacted the authorities to be told, "The case is under investigation. The whereabouts of the person is a secret."[6] This has become a common refrain, such as with Wang Quanzhang's wife, Li Wenzu, and his lawyers having been countlessly told on their attempts to contact Wang that no record for such a person exists.[7] In other cases, following six months of disappearance in RSDL, police have transferred individuals into criminal detention centers under false names in order to prolong the secrecy of their fate and whereabouts. When Chen Guiqiu found out that her husband, Xie Yang (Chapter 7), had been placed in RSDL, at first she didn't know what to expect but as she learned more she felt increasingly powerless:

They just took him and there is nothing anyone can do, at all.[8]

Much remains unknown, by definition, of this shadowy system that allows the police to detain anyone in total secret for up to six months, and potentially longer, without access to a lawyer or any legal recourse to challenge their incommunicado detention, an enforced disappearance. Torture is common. To dismantle such an abusive system of repression, greater understanding is necessary and that is precisely why this book is a vital contribution to not only our understanding of China's assault on human rights but also our broader understanding of authoritarian politics and state violence.

What China does arguably concerns everyone. China has proven that it is more than happy to share its repressive tactics with its neighbors, or to simply impose its will over them. What's more, the victims of RSDL have not just been Chinese citizens. Think of Taiwanese pro-democracy activist Lee Ming-che,[9] or the two Swedish citizens Peter Dahlin and Hong Kong bookseller Gui Minhai. In Gui's case, Chinese authorities went so far as to abduct him in October 2015 from inside Thailand before kidnapping him to mainland China, and placing him under RSDL. Gui Minhai's daughter, also a Swedish citizen, Angela Gui, didn't find out about her father for weeks.

I was expecting a call from him that never came... Three weeks after we were supposed to speak, my dad's colleague Lee Bo[10] emailed me saying my dad had been missing for over 20 days, and that he feared he'd been taken by 'Chinese special agents for political reasons.' He also told me that three of their other colleagues had gone missing... Because I still hadn't had any direct communication from Chinese authorities regarding my dad's detention, I didn't learn of the term Residential Surveillance at a Designated Location until fairly late.[11]

Residential Surveillance at a Designated Location is admittedly cumbersome even for a Chinese Communist Party euphemism. It appears in the amended CPL, which was adopted at the National People's Congress in March 2012, and entered into force on 1 January 2013. In a symbolic gesture of openness, a draft version had been released in August 2011 and opened for one month of public consultation in September. Tang Jitian (Chapter 1) recalls that when he first read about RSDL he feared it would be used to legalize secret detentions, as indeed it has been. He writes:

> It is an evil legislation. RSDL is worse than death for most of its victims.

As legal scholar Stanley Lubman pointed out in a *Wall Street Journal* op-ed in March 2012,[12] it is ironic that only days before the CPL was adopted, the human rights organization Chinese Human Rights Defenders, in its annual report, noted that 2011 had been a year characterized by the "extensive use of extralegal detention, and enforced disappearance and torture."[13] The UN Working Group on Enforced or Involuntary Disappearances declared it a "pattern of enforced disappearances in China, where persons suspected of dissent are taken to secret detention facilities."[14] Tang Jitian was one such victim. In his story in this book he compares the 2011 "pattern of enforced disappearances" with the 709 Crackdown in 2015:

> When I think about my condition in 2011, it was better than what is happening now. At that time, the authorities had to pay attention to voices from outside and inside China. But now, they have the law to protect them [referring to the legalization of enforced disappearances with RSDL]; they care less about any pressure from outside the country.

Beginning in the pre-dawn hours of 9 July 2015, China launched a coordinated strike against hundreds of Chinese human rights lawyers, legal assistants, activists, and family members in what has come to be known as the 709 Crackdown. It was the worst assault on civil society since the bloody suppression of the 1989 Democracy Movement. The initial targets included human rights lawyer Wang Yu (Chapter 3), her husband, Bao Longjun (Chapter 11), and partners at Beijing's Fengrui Law Firm, including Wang Quanzhang. Wang Yu recalls the night they came for her:

Without warning, the lights in my house were cut...

...I tried to phone for help, but before anyone could answer, someone had already broken through the door, and was instantly upon me. The light from his headlamp flashed into my face as he spoke, 'Don't move! We're from Beijing Public Security Bureau.'

Within days, the disappearances had spread around China, and later even crossed its borders. In October 2015, a few months after the abduction of his parents Wang Yu and Bao Longjun, the then 16-year-old Bao Zhuoxuan made a brave attempt to flee from persecution in China, accompanied by barefoot lawyer Xing Qingxian and rights defender Tang Zhishun (Chapter 9). But, soon after having crossed the border into Myanmar from China's Yunnan Province, they were apprehended by Chinese police in the tiny mountain town of Mongla. They were forced back into China and placed under RSDL.

I remember closely reading about this unfolding at the time because my organization, China Action, a year earlier had been supporting Xing Qingxian run a legal aid center in Sichuan. He had provided pro-bono legal support for victims of government abuse. And it was because of this past partnership that the police had accused Peter during his own period of RSDL of masterminding the attempt to smuggle Bao Zhuoxuan out of the country.

Tang Zhishun recalls with some irony the charges he was accused of soon after having been forced back from Myanmar and placed under RSDL:

They informed me that the charge against me had been changed from illegally crossing a national border to inciting subversion of state power. What a threat! They really overestimated me.

Disappearances under RSDL have been a common feature employed against those accused of subversion, lumping human rights defenders together with terror suspects. This much is known. But RSDL has also been used as a threat to coerce confessions or the denouncement of colleagues, proving the state employs it more as a tool of repression than by any stretch of the imagination as a legal procedure. Jiang Xiaoyu (Chapter 8) tells how he was abducted, held in secret, tortured, and threatened with disappearance for years if he didn't cooperate.

Not everyone knows how to prepare for being disappeared, and only more recently have human rights defenders in China begun making preemptive plans with family and lawyers in the event they lose their freedom. But even for those who know what to expect, it is no less traumatic. Chen Zhixiu (Chapter 4) recalls the mounting anxiety of preparing and expecting to be disappeared, so much so that he almost welcomed it when they finally came to take him:

> *Somehow, I felt relaxed when they arrived, standing there in my small rented apartment. I was surrounded by threatening security agents and yet I was kind of happy. I had been so nervous over the previous days, unable to really concentrate on anything other than remembering to always look over my shoulder... At least, when they burst into my apartment, I didn't have to be nervous about it anymore.*

Of course, even when you are expecting it, the act itself is violent and abrupt, whether you are disappeared for two nights, two months, or as in the case of Wang Quanzhang, at the time of writing, two years. An enforced disappearance is ongoing until the person's fate or whereabouts are known, and there is no minimum time period for an enforced disappearance.

I remember at one point in 2016, receiving a worried email from a rights defender who knew he was being monitored and feared the police would come for him. We agreed that I would periodically check on him over WhatsApp since I wasn't living in China anymore. One Friday, I messaged him. He was at work and leaving soon. He would be home in an hour. I messaged again. He was on the subway, this time he said he would be home in 40 minutes. I messaged again. He was about to get off the subway, and said he would be home in 20 minutes. I messaged again 20 minutes later, no reply. And again 30 minutes later, still no reply. An hour later, the silence had become excruciating. I knew he had been *taken*.

A few days later, I received a distraught and tearful voice message, followed by an email:

> *I am so scared. I am writing this email with my tears. I was beaten and questioned by State Security. They put a black bag over my head. They threatened to destroy my life, my family, my parents, everything. I know they can. Sorry, I can't hold myself together. I can't sleep. I can't eat. I am totally crushed. I could be taken again anytime. I don't know what to do. Please find a way to try and save other people. I don't know if I dare to write to you again.*[15]

During an enforced disappearance, the risk of torture is heightened, and indeed nearly every story in this book recounts some form of ill-treatment, from sleep deprivation and psychological trauma to threats against family and a range of physical torture.

As Teng Biao writes in the Foreword, the torture of many of the disappeared victims of the 709 Crackdown is now well documented. Even for those accustomed to the depravities of China's repression, the accounts of torture of human rights defenders, from Li Chunfu to Xie Yang (Chapter 7) are shocking. Such brutal accounts of RSDL led a group of 11 countries in early 2017 (conspicuously absent were the United States and European Union) to issue a joint statement demanding China investigate reports of torture and end the RSDL system.[16]

China, however, has responded to such condemnation by doubling down on the systematization of RSDL, and enforced disappearances. In its National Human Rights Action Plan (2016-2020), China stated: "Places of surveillance shall be regularized" and promised to "seriously [implement] the system of Residential Surveillance at a Designated Location."[17] Such vocabulary points to China's intention to expand RSDL. At the same time, cases such as Jiang Xiaoyu (Chapter 8), where RSDL was used purely as a coercive threat, are increasing alongside its use beyond even the vaguely written parameters in the law, with the police even abandoning superficial accusations of national security crimes. This can lead to only one conclusion: We have only seen the beginning of Residential Surveillance at a Designated Location.

This trajectory of repression is what makes the timing of this book so important. It not only seeks to unmask the systematic abuses of RSDL, it is also the first detailed depiction of RSDL as *experienced directly by its victims*. And it is exactly in its narrative richness that it offers new insight and understanding into the shadows of China's assault on human rights.

Michael Caster is a human rights advocate and researcher. He was one of the co-founders of the Chinese Urgent Action Working Group (China Action), a Beijing-based human rights organization that ran from 2009 until 2016. He holds a Master's in Conflict Studies and Human Rights from the University of Utrecht and a Masters of Law and Diplomacy from the Fletcher School at Tufts University.

Chapter 1
Dealing with the Devil | **TANG JITIAN**

Tang Jitian (唐吉田), male, born 1968, is one of China's most well-known rights defense lawyers. Originally from China's northeast, Tang began his legal career in southern China before relocating to Beijing. He has taken on many politically sensitive cases including representing rights defenders and Falun Gong practitioners. He also campaigned to end the hated Re-education Through Labor system (it was finally abolished in 2013).

As punishment for his rights defense, he has been detained, beaten, harassed, sent death threats, and been disappeared. In 2010, the government revoked Tang's lawyer's license, a common way to attack rights lawyers, but he continues to fight for human rights in China.

Tang Jitian's story is based on his own words, with additional material taken from an interview he gave for the Chinese-language book, *Jasmine Revolution in China: Stories of Repression and Persecution*, edited by Hua Ze, and published in 2015 in Taiwan.[1]

It was February 2011. I had been home in Jilin for the Spring Festival. [Human rights defender] Zhang Yongpan had contacted me about a video Chen Guangcheng [a famous blind lawyer who fled China in 2012] and his wife had secretly recorded on the horrors of their house arrest and ongoing surveillance and intimidation. Even though Chen Guangcheng had supposedly been released from prison five months earlier, he was not free. After they released that video, they were beaten pretty badly. The situation was quite urgent and something had to be done.

Concerned about Chen Guangcheng, I rushed back to Beijing. On the train, I received a call from [rights lawyer] Jiang Tianyong inviting me to a meeting to discuss what action we could take for Chen Guangcheng.

I arrived in Beijing around noon. I went immediately to meet Zhang Yongpan so we could go together to the meeting with the other lawyers. We were meeting at a hotpot restaurant. Once we got there, I noticed that State Security Agent Sun Di was waiting for me with some other agents. "It's difficult to find you," he said. "But we always have a way to locate you." He told me that he hoped we would cooperate more in the New Year. I responded bluntly that we have no reason to cooperate.

Inside the restaurant, Teng Biao and other rights lawyers were already there when I arrived. We spoke as we ate. I proposed a coordinated action. My strategy was that someone should go to visit Chen in Linyi. Others should stage a protest outside the Shandong Provincial Office in Beijing, while at the same time another group should report the case and file appeals.

We ate inside a private room at the restaurant. We knew State Security agents were sitting just outside eating at the crowded tables and joked that each lawyer was responsible for escorting his own assigned agent once we left. At one point, while we were eating, someone received a phone call from State Security telling him he was not allowed to attend the meeting, ordering him to leave immediately. The call was ignored.

Our lunchtime meeting finished around 3pm. Zhang Yongpan accompanied me to my house to pick up my things. I was supposed to move to a new place that a friend had rented to avoid suspicion. I knew I was under surveillance and wanted to change my residence.

We had barely arrived when some people started knocking at the door. They identified themselves as police from the local district police station. I refused to open the door. Zhang thought quickly and called Ye Jinghuan, a friend, to ask her to on hurry over. We were worried that we would be taken before Jinghuan arrived. I thought maybe they would put me in a detention center for a couple of days. I thought maybe they would escort me back to my hometown and forbid me from returning to Beijing for a while. I certainly didn't think they would put me in a secret prison, although I had already experienced that for a week back in 2009. I hadn't realized that things had become so serious.

It all happened so quickly. I hadn't taken it seriously enough to plan a lawyer for myself in case things got bad. It was a lesson for me, to always plan things in advance. When I look back today, I know now it should be a normal part of protection for every rights defender in China to have a lawyer in advance and to make plans with trusted friends and relatives to be ready with advocacy or other help when needed.

The knocking continued but we still didn't dare open the door. There was a horrible sound. I think they were trying to break down the door. And then, there was a new sound, a grating in the lock. They had called a locksmith. They got the door open in less than a minute.

Immediately, over a dozen policemen and plainclothes officers rushed into my apartment. At once they separated Zhang Yongpan and me. One of the officers asked me if I was Tang Jitian. I said that I was, and he ordered me to come with him. I admonished him. "How dare you. By what right do you just break down the door and take me away however you want." Ignoring me, he just dragged me outside.

As I was being removed from the apartment, I saw Zhang Yongpan was being pushed into the sofa. I was being dragged downstairs when Ye Jinghuan arrived. "Look at what they have done,"

I yelled. "They broke the lock to my door just like that!" She tried to approach but was pushed away by the police. Several officers dragged me into a waiting police car and we sped away.

When we arrived at the Guanganmen Police Station, I was immediately locked into a small room with a guard, an older man who chain-smoked the whole time. The room was very smoky.

A short while later, I could hear Zhang Yongpan shouting in the other room. "How can you just casually abduct people like this?" I overheard the police yelling at him to be smart and think about his situation. There was a lot of loud fighting at first but after a while I couldn't hear anything. It wasn't until much later, after I was released and free from constant surveillance, that I was finally able to meet with him again, but by then we didn't speak much about that afternoon at the police station.

A few hours passed.

Two tough looking younger guards came into the room and dragged me away by my arms. Outside, two cars were waiting. A few State Security officers, who identified themselves as being from the First Bureau of State Security, hurried me into the back seat of one of the waiting cars. I was crammed into the middle, with two people on either side. One of them ordered me to cooperate. He confiscated everything from my pockets. They slipped a black plastic bag over my head, and we were on our way.

It was the kind of plastic shopping bag you get from the market. They were very strict about it, making sure that my mouth and nose were both inside. They didn't just put the bag over my head but also pushed my face into the gap between the two seats in front of me. Without much space to breathe, I worried that I would suffocate. I felt dizzy.

I was still wearing my down jacket. I had gone directly to the restaurant from the train station, where I had come from my hometown, which is much colder than Beijing, and then home, where they took me before I had a chance to change. My head was covered by a plastic bag, back bent forward, head pushed against the seat; the position was really uncomfortable. I tried to shift but they didn't allow me to move, just pushed me harder. I asked if I could take off my jacket, mostly to breathe better, but they refused.

The car drove on for over an hour. At first, I could hear the sounds of cars crossing on the highway, which gave way to the sound of tractors. I realized that we were now in the countryside.

It was after 9pm when the car stopped in a courtyard. The person in front of me got out of the car, making commands as he left: "Watch him. Don't let him move." Maybe 20 minutes passed before I was taken inside. I still couldn't see anything because of the bag over my head but it felt like we were walking down a corridor. They sat me in a chair and pulled the bag off my head. I could see that they had sat me facing a wall. There was a lamp in front of me. The light was shining directly into my eyes. One of the State Security agents locked me into handcuffs. He told another guard to monitor me, to make sure I wasn't allowed to move, and then left the room.

I had sweated so much in the car, but after a while sitting shackled in the room, I started to feel cold. I asked the guard to allow me to use the toilet. He must not have been able to think for himself because he had to go ask for instructions. He came back with several people to unlock my handcuffs and led me to the toilet.

The whole time I was in their custody, I was never allowed to close a toilet door when I used it. There was always a guard watching me. I noticed that anything that would help identify the place, like soaps with a hotel name or address, toothbrush or other toiletries had all been removed. I would not be allowed to brush my teeth or take a shower for many days.

The place looked like a countryside resort. The room where I was held was quite large and had two beds but they had created a triangular space for me between a bed, the closet, and a table. My movements were limited to the triangular space. If I had to use the toilet, they would move the long table a little to let me out.

They had already set up this furniture cage before I arrived. When they put me inside the triangle, they adjusted it a little to make it smaller. It was just a threat, to make me feel scared from the outset. They were just showing me their power. I had this kind of experience with them before. I knew that I would not be getting out of this place anytime soon. I accepted the situation but felt really nervous.

Four guards took turns monitoring me. The first team was very young, with Henan and Sichuan accents. The man with the Sichuan accent warned me to be more cooperative, otherwise I would suffer.

Not until 11pm did they bring in some food. They gave me some *laobing* [baked pancake] and a few pieces of kale. I didn't feel much like eating but had a few bites. Afterwards, they continued to force me to sit silently and without moving, straight upright on the hard chair. If I tried to lean back a little, someone would kick my feet and shout at me. I had a slipped disc from some time before. I felt extreme pain after a while and, explaining that I had lower back problems, asked to change my position. They didn't even bother to respond. My nose started to run. I asked for a tissue paper. They thought I was a real troublemaker.

The next day was Lantern Festival. They took me to another room after breakfast, again with the black plastic bag over my head.

My new room was similar to the previous one, but the distance between the bed and the wall was a little shorter. They could make a triangular area just by using a table and a bed. I sat inside the corner they had constructed for me. The second room felt colder. They kept the curtains closed to block out the sunlight.

That night, I heard fireworks from the village celebrating the Lantern Festival. I knew there were people outside. I wasn't alone. I felt a little better.

Sometimes I had conversations with the guards. An older guard, who told me that he had taken the bar exam, asked me why I was being detained. "No reason, I just told some truths that the officials don't like." He seemed genuinely interested, and asked what the outcome might be. I explained that I might be sentenced. He and his partner were nicer. When they saw that I had a runny nose they offered me cold medicine. At night when I was supposed to sit straight in that uncomfortable position, they would look the other way so I could slouch a little and be more comfortable.

Most of the interrogation sessions followed the same pattern: two or three State Security officers spoke with me and tried to entrap me. They asked how I came to start working in the human rights field and who recommended or introduced me to it. They would ask with whom did I keep in touch with or cooperate with the most? How do we contact each other? What diplomats or foreign friends or journalists do I speak with? How and what do we discuss? They asked about specific cases, what my role had been, or which family members of clients I had contacted. I tried to only give information for those who had already left, such as foreigners, or only basic information. For those who were still active, I didn't mention anything. They were particularly interested in how lawyers cooperate and communicate, and find outside support.

A few days after Lantern Festival, an officer came in to speak with me, similar to the others. I told him I wouldn't talk with an unidentified person. He told me his family name was Li and he was from State Security. When he entered, the guard watching me left the room. Li told me that he had researched my situation and my past, and had gone to my middle school, high school, university, and my former workplaces. He said that all of my old classmates, colleagues, teachers, and bosses had good impressions of me, that I had had such a bright future. Why had I stepped on to this road? I told him that everyone has different interests, just that his opinion was different from mine.

He brought up that I had defended Falun Gong practitioners. I told him that it is okay to disagree with their beliefs or to criticize their actions, but that you can't violate their basic rights on principle. I explained that I was just defending their basic rights. He tried talking about Tibet and Xinjiang, pressing me to reveal my opinions about these sensitive issues. I told him that my only concern was about human rights. It doesn't matter what ethnic group is involved, everyone's basic rights must be protected. He changed tactics.

Li threatened my children, and my relatives' children. The way he talked about them made me think that he had researched them all. It made me believe that they could do anything. In China, State Security can extend their hands anywhere they want. They have many ways. I knew I hadn't done anything wrong. Even if they put me in jail, I had no reason to feel ashamed. But, objectively, I thought about it bringing trouble for my family. How shameless the police are! It made me very angry. I had been doing what I believed in for many years. Just because I didn't give up my beliefs, kept to my principles, in the end I was bringing trouble to the people around me. It made me feel anxious and guilty, and extremely conflicted.

Starting the day after the Lantern Festival, there were some times when they didn't give me breakfast. The food they gave me for lunch and dinner was very simple: some rice, sometimes *laobing*. The two younger guards thought I was making too much trouble for them by going to the toilet so they limited the amount of water I was allowed to drink.

The older guards treated me better. Sometimes they would share their hot water with me. But after a few days I overheard some of the guards talking quietly outside the door. The nice older guard was going to be transferred back to the city. I assumed it was because he had not been strict enough with me. I never saw him again.

On the 21st, a State Security officer came into my room around 7 or 8 in the evening. His name was Zhao and he had the airs of a former soldier who never shed his old vulgar habits and strict manner. He was tough but surprisingly honest. Likely trying to feign closeness, he called the Party a bandit, saying that our country had been founded on a mountain of the dead and that anyone who wanted to take it away must to be prepared to lose their head. Talking about the law is a waste of time, he continued. It would be simple to dig a hole and bury you alive or make you disappear or arrange a car accident, he threatened.

He issued these threats with such fluid composure, as if he was extremely familiar with such things. As he finished speaking, he shouted an order outside. Four men with closely cut hair, tall and strong, ran into the room. They looked like they had been well trained. They saluted Zhao. "Ready Sir, awaiting instructions!" He ordered them to take me outside.

These four guys were armed police [the People's Armed Police, a vast paramilitary force in China]. It seemed the military had taken over my case. Again, they slipped a black plastic bag over my head and took me away. My head was pushed in between the two front seats in the car as before. We must have driven for about two or three hours before arriving at another countryside villa.

The new place had very bad living conditions. The room was small. The two beds were pressed almost together. There was no toilet seat. I had to use a water ladle to scoop water to clean the toilet after using it.

I was made to sit up straight, facing the wall in a tiny space. One light shone brightly, directly into my face. The air conditioner was on, blowing cold air on me, even though it was winter. They wore big cotton padded coats. I had sweated a lot on the way there, crammed into the car between the guards, with my head in a plastic bag and wearing my thick jacket. My jacket was so wet with sweat I couldn't wear it anymore.

At this new place, the four armed police and two younger guards took turns monitoring me. They made sure I knew who was in charge, saying, "Our soldiers only take orders from the top. If you don't behave, we will break your kneecaps." I wasn't allowed to sleep. I was cold and tired. It was hard to sit still. If I didn't sit properly, they would kick me.

The armed police did not wear uniforms. Listening to them speak, it was clear they were real brutes, former military perhaps, happy to dispatch discipline and violence. They smoked a lot, side-by-side. In the confined environment, because of the smoke swirling inside the room, I was coughing non-stop.

The second day after I was transferred, there was a sudden power outage. One of the guards went outside. There must have been some confusion because I remember seeing an electrician come in but then everyone was yelling. The leader was criticizing the guards and the electrician. The electrician had seen me. I guess nobody was supposed to know I was there.

This place looked like a normal resort, from the outside and how it was decorated inside, just like the type of place people might go for a weekend vacation. I guessed that the staff at this resort had no idea I was being held here. Maybe because the electrician had seen me, the next day I was transferred again.

Maybe they were moving me so often as a better way to keep my location a secret, or to play with my mind, to break my faith and to scare me, or to make me cooperate with them and make a deal.

This time when they moved me, they covered my head with a black hood made from cotton, a real black hood. Compared with the plastic bag, it felt better; it was more comfortable. But I was still quite opposed to wearing it, because wearing a black hood means being controlled and humiliated. I was angry. But since I was under such strict control, I couldn't say or do anything.

Again, we drove for two to three hours before we arrived. I overheard my captors speaking vaguely about the name of the place. After my release, I tried to search for it based on what I remembered but I couldn't be sure.

The new place was a suite. It must originally have had three beds in the room but they had taken one away. The window was not only covered by a curtain, but they had also propped up a mattress to block out the light. I assume that they had set up the room before they transferred me there because there's no way it was already like that.

Soon after we arrived at the new location, they started to make me do military drills. An armed police officer demonstrated how to squat, stand to attention, stand at ease, turn, and salute; each position requiring precise movements and timing. When I squatted, I had to put two hands behind my neck and keep my body straight. I had to practice folding a blanket to a right angle, like the shape of tofu. This was not easy for me. The hardest part for me was practicing giving military salutes to my captors.

Their purpose was to break my determination, to make me accept their power. They sometimes use this kind of military training on detainees they don't like. The armed police in China only have strong bodies, but very simple minds.

My body couldn't stand it anymore. They were going to beat me. I told them that I was done. I couldn't do any more exercises. I told them to go ask their boss for instructions, that they could punish me however they wanted but I wasn't doing any more training.

That evening, two security agents came in and asked if I had anything to tell them. I shot back, just tell me what you want me to say. They allowed me to sit. They explained that I had fallen onto the wrong path. Many things I had done had crossed the line. They said their big boss was very angry with me. "Who do you think orders the armed police?" He meant their big boss was from the top levels of the Party.

He pointed out that I was technically still a Communist Party member and used to be a cadre. It sounded like they were saying I was cheating the Party.

He said that the Party was trying to help me now, otherwise I would end up disappeared like [persecuted rights lawyer] Gao Zhisheng or [dissident] Liu Xiaobo, who would be an old man when he was finally released from prison [Liu Xiaobo died in prison in July 2017]. I had never met either of them. Both of them, despite the international attention on their cases, got in trouble with the state. They were forcibly disappeared and imprisoned. I am not as well-known as them, which means if they wanted to do anything to me, they would not have much to consider. All this was used to pressure me. My mind was racing. When will my resistance give out? I was trying to calculate what I had to gain or lose.

Even if I had the ability to gather together a group of people to oppose the Party, the Party has all the money and guns. If I didn't cooperate, they would dig a hole and bury me alive. Who would find me? Even if I could get out, I might also have a "car accident" or "commit suicide." My only hope now, they explained, was to cooperate.

To intimidate me, they asked if I wanted to know about Teng Biao's and Jiang Tianyong's situation. I could tell from the faces of my interrogators that Teng Biao and Jiang Tianyong were being kept somewhere by other agents of the state, perhaps being treated in the same way. They mentioned someone named Li Jinping, a former policeman, who had gone mad through torture. It was a way to threaten me.

I had so many concerns. Since I was disappeared for so many days, my family must have been very nervous. My parents weren't in good health. But I knew how State Security operates. They just needed a so-called good result to report to their superiors. After that, what I did was not their concern. I was coughing a lot those days and could see some blood mixed with the phlegm. I knew I might get an infection if things continued. I would certainly break down. I asked to hear their conditions.

I was not allowed to contact foreign media, foreign embassies, human rights NGOs, and not even allowed to have contact with Chinese petitioners or some of my friends. I felt like I was dealing with the devil. My feelings were complicated. It is hard to describe them.

I agreed to their deal on the night of 22 February. The guard brought a blanket and let me rest on the mattress. They allowed me to have a shower the next day. I assumed it was because they were tired of my body's sourness since I had been sweating and wearing the same clothes the whole time but hadn't been allowed to shower. One soldier took my clothes to be washed. That night, while I was asleep, I overheard a guard speaking about how could someone who had led such a big movement be dressed so shabbily.

They told me to list everything I had been involved with: the people I was in contact with, the cases I had represented. I listed all my public activities except for anything that might have hurt others; for those, I said I couldn't remember any details.

They were not happy with my list a few times. They told me not to play word games; saying if I were going to pretend I should do a better job of it otherwise their big boss would become angry again.

I tried my best not to cause any trouble for my friends and colleagues. It was several days, maybe 24 or 25 February before the police seemed happy with what I had written. They told me to make a document, listing the things I promised I would not do and those I promised I would do.

I promised to participate in Party activities because I was still a Party member. I promised not to be in touch with old friends. I promised to toe the government's line, to report to State Security when

I came to Beijing, and not to accept any interviews or to contact foreign media.

Even after writing the document, they still woke me up at 5am every day. I was made to go through the military drills. I wasn't allowed to sleep until 10pm. My body was weak. I felt nauseous and vomited when I brushed my teeth.

Eventually the armed police started to treat me better. They told me this was just what they had to do to make a living and asked me to forgive them for the things they had done to me. Taking pity on me, they tried to convince me to lead a good life, to earn some money, and not get involved anymore with this sensitive business.

On maybe 26 or 27 February, someone from the Ministry of Public Security leadership came to see me. He told me that they had already reported to their big boss, who was satisfied with what I had written. I was thinking, imagining, how much fear this man, in his 60s, must feel in front of his boss.

I had to read my list of promises in front of a camera. They recorded it with a handheld camera. I remember we had to do two takes. There were some guards and officers as always but also someone who identified himself as Meng from the University of Political Science and Law, and a few others in senior positions, including Director Jiang. The video took at least an hour to record.

On 4 March, State Security came to explain that I couldn't stay in Beijing and that I had to return to my hometown. If I agreed to leave Beijing, I would have my freedom back. I realized that if I refused and tried to stay in Beijing anyway, I would be under constant surveillance and wouldn't be able to do anything. I also needed to consider my health, which was deteriorating. I agreed to go back to my hometown. That evening the armed police left, leaving me in the care of just two guards.

The next morning, they returned all the things they had confiscated from me. They put a black hood over my head again and drove to the airport. I was escorted back to my hometown by four State Security agents, along with Director Jiang, Meng and several of the senior level officials present during the video recording.

Director Jiang sat in first class. The rest of us were in economy. After more than 20 days of secret detention, finally I would be able to see the sunshine, to breathe fresh air.

We arrived in my hometown, Yanji, at around 1pm. The Vice Director of the local Public Security and three State Security officers were waiting at the airport. All the police met and exchanged greetings and then the four who had escorted me from Beijing left with the leader of the local police.

The officers took me to Yanji police station. They reprimanded me. They were mostly concerned that I would bring them trouble. Since they wanted me to cooperate, I told them all about how I was kidnapped in Beijing, including how I was black hooded. I told them about my detention. I remember I said I didn't know why they had treated me the way they had. I couldn't think of anything according to the law to warrant my treatment. They wrote down everything I told them.

The day before the Beijing agents left Yanji, they called me to meet them at a teahouse. They were angry that I had spoken with the local police; they were angry about what I had told them. I said I had just been cooperating with the police. They told me not to tell anyone else about what had happened during my disappearance. The warning was from their big boss. They explained I should stay away from Beijing until after the 18th Communist Party Congress [that November] otherwise I would be punished. They gave me a phone number. I was to call them in case of anything.

They returned my phone when I was released. I checked my call list. I saw that even after I was taken, that phone had been used to call my friends. I was afraid that the police were phishing my friends or trying to trick them. I didn't contact anyone directly, just changed my phone. This was a mistake. I should have contacted them to find out what the police had said. If I had done so I could have helped them by warning them. It is important to set a better password for your phone, to avoid this kind of mistake in the future, I realized. I know now I should delete messages regularly and not give police easy access to evidence or information that could put other people at risk.

For some time after I was released, I didn't have a problem sleeping but I struggled to have an appetite. I had contracted pulmonary tuberculosis. While I was inside, I lost a lot of weight and after I was first released many friends saw that I was so emaciated, that my face was grey and my spirit gone. They joked that I looked like someone back from a cremation or funeral parlor. While I was inside, I would sometimes cough up blood but when I told the guards they didn't care. They just responded by saying that the bleeding wouldn't kill me. I had to seek medical treatment for two years after I was released.

The emotional impact of detention is sometimes even stronger than the physical impact; it can take a long time to resolve. It doesn't go away overnight.

Later, when I first read about the new Criminal Procedure Law and article 73 [on RSDL], I thought it was a way to legalize and regularize secret detention, such as they did to me in 2011. It is an evil legislation. RSDL is worse than death for most of its victims. There were a lot of voices from inside China and abroad calling for this article to be removed but unfortunately since 2012, China's legislation has focused on limiting citizen's rights even though they barely had any to begin with.

When I think about my condition in 2011, it was better than what is happening now. At that time, the authorities had to pay attention to voices from outside and inside China. But now, they have the law to protect them; they care less about any pressure from outside the country.

My detention in 2011, strictly speaking, was not the same as Residential Surveillance. There was an article about Residential Surveillance in the old Criminal Procedure Law, but it had a specific procedure. Now that they have added this "Designated Location" the legislation is ridiculous. They want to legalize all their evil acts and force people to accept them. The new law is unacceptable and does not have any natural legitimacy. In the last few years of my legal practice, I have felt that my earlier concerns were justified. The enormous number of RSDL cases, especially from 2015, is proof that this legislation is outrageous, evil, and cruel.

Chapter 2
A place where the law does not exist | LIU SHIHUI

Liu Shihui (刘士辉), male, born 1966, is a lawyer and long-time human rights defender based in China's southern Guangdong province. Originally from Inner Mongolia in northern China, he started practicing law in 2000. The authorities have barred him from renewing his lawyer's license since 2010 because of his rights defense work.

On 20 February 2011, security forces brutally assaulted Liu as he attempted to photograph a gathering in Guangzhou connected with calls for a "Jasmine Revolution" in China. Days later they placed him under Residential Surveillance, and deported his Vietnamese wife. Even after he was released, the authorities continued to persecute him, including disappearing him during the 2015 "709 Crackdown."

In 2011, waves of "Jasmine Revolutions" had spread all over the world, subverting several dictatorships in their wake. It seemed unavoidable that it wouldn't reach China—the greatest dictatorship remaining in the world. By 20 February that year, the idea for a "China Jasmine Revolution Day" had spread on Twitter. The meeting points in different cities were shared inside and outside of "the wall" [China's Great Firewall which blocks many popular overseas websites]. In Guangzhou, my city, the meeting point was set for Renmin Park.

At noon that day, I posted my last Twitter message. "I have a date with Miss Jasmine. The location is Guangzhou Renmin Park. The time is 2pm on 20 February. I'm not seeking privacy. You are welcome to come and have a look." After posting that, I left my house with my camera.

I was walking down the road when suddenly a hand as hard as iron pliers grabbed hold of my throat and pushed me to the side of the road, while at the same time, someone tried to place a white bag over my head, a garbage bag of some kind. I tried to push them away, only to see another four to five men, all black-clad, all very strong looking, with clubs in their hands, coming out from a beige-colored minivan next to me.

I had been attacked before by men not in uniform, and instinctively knew these were Domestic Security officers. They attacked me. I was pushed onto and over a pile of bricks on the side of the road, high enough that it blocked the view of most passersby. The group kicked, punched, and attacked me with their clubs. The clubs must have hit every part of my body. I was screaming: "Help!" and trying to protect myself with my hands, but to little avail. It went on for a few minutes before they stopped. A dirty hand reached down to grab the newly purchased Nikon camera flung around my back, and as soon as they had it, they ran off. I felt like I was half in a coma, unable to move. I tried to get back on my feet and chase after them, but didn't stand a chance. They all jumped into a minivan and sped off.

I scoured the site of the attack, picking up anything they had left for possible evidence: a 1m bamboo club and the white bag they tried to use as a hood over my head. I called 110—the police—right away. I knew filing a report was ridiculous, like reporting the right hand's offense to the left, but I wanted to file anyway. I went to the hospital.

At the time, the weather in Guangzhou was even colder than the political climate. I wore three layers of pants. Most of the bleeding was from my left leg, a cut 3cm long, 1cm deep, like an open mouth, blood flowing continuously, soaking everything. If it hadn't been winter, if I hadn't worn so many layers, I can't image how bad it would have been. After the checkup, besides violent pain and bruising on many parts of my body, they also said I had muscle damage in one shoulder, blood in my urine, and a damaged spleen. I had stiches for the wound in my left leg; to this day the scar is very visible. They said they didn't find any fractures, but I had my doubts. I'll get back to this later.

Soon after, my friend arrived at the hospital, and took photos of the injuries I had sustained. By then, information on the attack had already started spreading over the internet. Friend after friend came by the hospital. I told the police about the incident. They took notes, and then they asked me who I thought was responsible.

"Guangzhou Domestic Security Police," I said. Their faces, their expressions, changed as if they had heard something unbelievable. It was obvious that they later tried to avoid handling my case. After midnight, they came to my house, loudly knocking on my door, apparently to "investigate the situation." I had already given them the evidence I had collected; the club and the plastic bag. I wrote down a request for them to check the security cameras in the area. It all happened near an intersection and there were plenty of cameras. They ignored it. I felt both angry and helpless at the same time. It was like dealing with a cat that is colluding with the mouse to support the chase.

On the afternoon of the 24 February, I was at the Guangdong Provincial Hospital; my medical records had "disappeared." I could sense something was going to happen, but could do nothing but return home. I prepared and updated my computer and placed the evidence and relevant information in the right place, after which I went to bed. The next day the United States Consul was coming to my house, as had been arranged by the Consulate in Guangzhou earlier that day.

About 2am, not long after I had managed to fall asleep, I was woken up by violent and loud smashing noises; someone was trying to break down the front door. Then I heard a loud voice cry out: "Liu Shihui, we are the Guangzhou Domestic Security Police. Open the door!"

I knew this spelled disaster, but I had no way out and nowhere to hide. I had no choice; I had to face whatever was coming. I turned on the light and put on some clothes. They continued hammering at the door; they were so loud it sounded as if they were tearing down the whole building. The room filled with dust, making it hard to breathe. I stayed near the bed, holding my wife, who I had just married. Having seen me beaten, she was already scared and was crying, doing all she could to help me. Fortunately, she was already clothed or I couldn't imagine how she would have felt when these monsters came through the door; I couldn't imagine how she could have faced these brutes if she had been naked in bed.

More than a dozen uniformed police rushed in as soon as the door came off. "We are the Guangzhou Domestic Security Police," they said, adding they were investigating me and my wife on suspicion of inciting subversion of state power. I explained over and over that my wife is not even Chinese, that she is from Vietnam, and doesn't speak a word of Chinese. There was no point involving her. They didn't listen, and didn't even go through any legal formalities when they took her.

She ended up spending 17 days in detention, before being forcibly deported from China.

The search lasted about two hours. They turned the whole place upside down. They didn't miss a thing, not a single piece of paper. They took all my paperwork, my laptop, the phones, USBs, books, case files, and more, even my electronic stock tracker. I had a copy of a poetry collection on the Tiananmen Massacre laid out and arranged as beautifully as I could. They grabbed it all and messed it up, perhaps the most heartbreaking moment of when they took my belongings.

I was taken to a nearby police station. The police announced: "You are being placed under Residential Surveillance on suspicion of inciting subversion of state power." I refused to sign their forms. At around 4 or 5 in the early morning I was pushed into a police car and handcuffed. As the car drove along, I tried to notice the road signs, to try to identify where they were taking me. They ended up taking me to a building called "Guangzhou Baiyun Police Training Center."

As I was taken into the building, I saw many sentries and guards around the gates.

They took me to the third floor, to a room that looked like a standard hotel room. There were two beds inside, one for me, and another for whichever guard whose turn it was to sleep. This room would be my cell and my interrogation chamber. There was one camera set at the front, recording 24 hours a day. The curtain over the window was thick and always closed; there would be no sunlight. Two fluorescent lights on the ceiling were kept on day and night. There were two to three guards in the room at all times, working in two and three shifts per day.

At 7am the next day, the interrogations began. I refused to answer their questions, saying: "You [Domestic Security Police] are the ones who attacked me." I requested to be allowed to go back to the hospital. I had one more checkup and test already paid for. Not surprisingly, they said no. To this day, the symptom I was supposed to have checked still remains; a numbness in my forefinger and thumb. It gets worse in cold weather.

"If you cooperate, there won't be any problems. If you don't, even if your hand is broken, you deserve it! In fact, not just your hand, your life can be broken."

This was what "Smiling Tiger," the leader of the Guangzhou Public Security Counterterrorism Section, told me. Throughout my time in interrogation and Residential Surveillance, I met many Domestic

Security Police, but none of them gave their names. I remember them by the nicknames I gave them.

Smiling Tiger was similar in age to me. He was often abrasive and threatening. The others claimed he was the leader, so his manner matched his position. It seemed the authorities equated a "Jasmine Revolution" with terrorism.

"Chief Li" might have been six or seven years younger than me. He was from Guangdong and spoke Cantonese. He was, maybe, 170cm tall, and said he was the leader of the Domestic Security Police unit here. I heard a guard outside my room addressing him as Chief Li, so I assume Li was his real name. He too, as a leader, was tough and ruthless.

"Mr. Tall, Rich, and Handsome" was probably less than 30 years old, tall, with fair skin and good-looking. He spoke Cantonese and claimed to have studied at the Beijing Police College. With his gentle demeanor and many jokes, he often played the role of the "good cop".

"Pre-trial Liang" was a few years older than me and he led pre-trial investigations for cases handled by the Guangzhou Public Security Bureau. He claimed he had graduated from Southwest University of Political Science and Law. He was violent, and was the only one to tell me his family name; all the others treated their identities as if they were state secrets.

Besides these, there were "Dumpy" from Guangzhou, who also spoke Cantonese, a low-ranking police officer from Xinjiang, and a bespectacled 30-something year old from Ningxia. He spoke with a heavy accent. The Ningxia man had a bad temper and often spoke in profanities.

In the beginning, I reacted with silence when the police interrogated and reprimanded me.

Smiling Tiger said: "You only have a few people with you who dare to subvert the state. My regime [the Communist Party of China] was built on the lives of three million."

They wanted me to confess my crime. "I didn't commit any crime, and I didn't subvert the Communist Party regime." When he saw that I would not open my mouth, Chief Li started shouting at me.

"Why didn't we take any of the others? Why did we just take you? You should understand your position. You are now a criminal, or why would the Domestic Security Police take you? We are here to protect the regime, to deal with your kind of hostile force. Why couldn't you just be happy being a lawyer? You had to place yourself in our way. Don't blame us for being cruel. You think we can't get evidence? How about we hold you for the next 10 years?"

I said I had committed no crime. At worst, I was just a suspect. "I wanted to be happy being a lawyer, but you already deprived me, illegally, of my license back in 2010."

Chief Li admonished me. "Do you think *you* can decide if you have committed a crime or not? Do you want to be tough like Yang Maodong? [Another human rights lawyer better known under his pen name Guo Feixiong]. Yang will be released soon. I'm telling you, we will make him suffer until he dies!" They were well aware of our close relationship, and how I tried to help him when he was sentenced to prison.

Even though it's been six years since that afternoon, I can still vividly remember the ruthlessness of his face when Chief Li said they would make Yang Maodong "suffer until he dies."

I had posted more than a dozen Twitter messages. That was their first evidence of me inciting subversion. I had organized Jasmine Revolution activities. Later they accused me of being the first to forward messages about it. Second, I had participated in discussions about a Jasmine Revolution. Third, I had participated in an activity to put slogans on T-shirts. The slogan on my T-shirt read: "One Party dictatorship anywhere, disaster everywhere." Fourth, I had participated in a commemoration for the Tiananmen Massacre. Fifth, I had accepted interviews with foreign media more than 20 times. Sixth, they said I had written several articles, amounting to inciting subversion of state power.

They printed out more than a dozen Twitter posts, and showed me several photos taken at meetings in Guangzhou. Based on this, they wanted me to admit to organizing a Jasmine Revolution. I laughed at their choice of words, "organize." All the information came from social media and foreign media, and all I had done was forward the information.

A fat officer interjected: "Why did you sell your stocks before the date of the Jasmine Revolution? Wasn't it so you could use the money to wage revolution?"

"I did it because I thought they would fall in value," I answered. "Why would I use my own money to start a revolution? I'm not that stupid." They had printed out my financial records.

When they couldn't find any evidence to prove I had organized any Jasmine Revolution activities, they returned to accusing me of being the first person to start forwarding information about it. No matter what I did, I couldn't get out of this.

While I was being beaten, and later detained and taken into Residential Surveillance, around 100 people had been targeted across the country, but it seemed I was the only one to be beaten to a bloody pulp. This, combined with them alleging that I had been organizing a revolution, meant they really thought I had played a key role. They didn't hesitate to beat me whenever they wanted.

They kept on admonishing and screaming at me. Evening finally arrived, but the interrogation continued. They took turns, two interrogators at a time, changing teams every few hours. After midnight, I requested to be allowed to rest.

"Do you think this is a hotel? You should understand your place!"

When I mentioned my wound as the reason for needing a rest, they simply said it was nothing compared to losing my life.

Even if I was a suspect, I had rights. The police should follow the law. Smiling Tiger said: "Do you think the US follows the law for those held in Guantanamo?"

"Do you think the Nationalists [KMT] talked about following the law when fighting the Communists? How can we talk about the law with you?"

I wasn't allowed to sleep the first night, or the second, or the third. If they weren't interrogating me, they would force me to sit on a chair, and even that was exhausting after a long time. I would nod off sometimes. The police would slam the table next to me and yell at me. My leg kept swelling, and the pain in my chest grew. I didn't know how long I could tolerate it.

"Exhausting an eagle" is an expression that is used to describe extended sleep deprivation. I knew about this torture technique. Since it was usually reserved for serious crimes under Chinese law, I didn't come across it much. It was from an older time. I had rarely seen or heard of any client who had suffered it, and in the rare cases they had, it was usually for a day or, at most, two.

I realized I was in a place where the law does not exist, a black hole, a camp controlled by monsters.

I knew it was useless but I still said I wanted to hire a lawyer. Chief Li said, "No suspects in this case are allowed to have a lawyer; it's been decided by the higher ups, so you better quit thinking about it."

I continued: "The procuratorate should supervise this investigation." Having said it I felt funny, having mentioned the prosecutor's oversight when I was inside a Black Jail with no connection to the outside world. Even if the prosecutor's office knew about me, it was useless, since both branches are controlled by the Party.

Smiling Tiger often said: "What's wrong with having a few people die to protect our regime? Your injury is nothing compared with losing your life. There's only a few of you that want to subvert state power."

I can never forget his cruel expression when he said that. I believed that what Smiling Tiger said was not just a threat but if necessary, if the order came, he would have happily killed me. These professional lackeys lost their humanity long ago.

I was nearly falling apart. I had spent several days without sleep, being constantly threatened, told off, and shouted at. A fourth and fifth night came and went, and I still wasn't allowed to sleep. I started getting dizzy; I developed tinnitus and a splitting headache. The pain was hard to describe. It was worse than just physical pain. I had physical trouble before, plus with the injuries from the attack, it was just unbearable and getting worse day by day. I knew they wanted to torture me as badly as they could, to gain complete power and control over me. I didn't know where the limit lay; how much could I take or how far would they push. Five days of this torture passed but I hadn't broken; at least I had kept my conscience clean.

After the sixth day, and more interrogations, my energy gave out. It was over. I collapsed; the police were finally forced to call in a doctor. After the doctor had checked me over, he whispered something to Chief Li, and they let me sleep. I was too weak to take off my clothes, and only with help could I remove my pants. I was always skinny, but now it was more than usual, and my left leg had swollen tremendously.

The police accused me of being the first one to forward information about the Jasmine Revolution, and of actively inciting others to take to the streets. I explained that Twitter is blocked by the government and very few people know how to climb the wall [by using a VPN or proxy to cross China's Great Firewall], and therefore no real danger could come from me forwarding information on Twitter.

The police asked how did I know that people inside China couldn't see the content? "Our technical department provides us data. There are some 500,000 people 'climbing the wall' every day." Although I knew that more and more people had started "climbing the wall," when I heard that number I was really surprised. If Guangzhou had 500,000 people using a VPN or proxies, how about Beijing, Shanghai, or Shenzhen? How many were there from all over the country? The police unintentionally leaked such an important state secret to me.

To make me confess, the police used various tactics besides sleep deprivation.

For example, in the beginning they would try to trick me. They said, "You are not a murderer; your crime is minor in comparison. If you can tell us about it, you will be fine." I wasn't fooled that easily, and didn't take the bait. In response, they switched tactics completely. Now they said that even though I hadn't murdered anyone, my situation was far more serious. "If your anti-Party activity had succeeded, millions would have died." The way they spoke sounded like something from the Cultural Revolution. When I pointed out that my "activities" had been perfectly legal, their response was, "How dare you! If your activities were successful, wouldn't you be in my position, and I would be in yours?"

While I was suffering those days and nights of sleep deprivation, the officers would often taunt me: "You should be satisfied. The food is good here. You have a bed by yourself, much better than any detention center." I felt more and more of my body and mind being consumed with fighting tiredness so that I was falling apart. I told Chief Li I'd like to be arrested, sent to a real detention center.

Detention centers could be cruel places for sure, but at least there were some institutional constraints, some safeguards, legal obligations that couldn't be so easily ignored. At least this kind of sleep deprivation would be hard if not impossible in a detention center.

"You deserve to stay here, there is no way you can go to a detention center. A detention center is too good for you," Chief Li shouted hoarsely.

Between 2009 and 2017, I have been in Residential Surveillance, administrative detention, criminal detention, and a Black Jail. Even though some of those treatments were harsh, my time in Residential Surveillance stands out as the worst, a system designed for prisoners of conscience, a place designed for torture.

The People's Republic of the Disappeared

After my newlywed wife was taken with me in the same raid, she was also placed in Residential Surveillance on suspicion of inciting subversion of state power. The police interrogated me: "Why did you travel to Vietnam? Who did you meet with? Did she come here with you to subvert Communist Party rule?" I couldn't help but laugh at such ridiculous allegations. I explained, again and again, that my wife didn't know about my work and that she didn't even speak Chinese. After seven or eight days, they must have known my wife knew nothing about these allegations. They should have released her, to keep her solely as a hostage was utterly illegal. They ignored my request [to release her] of course.

I was so angry that they had kidnapped her. I demanded to know how the police could be so cruel as to destroy a marriage. They answered perfunctorily: "We hope you can stay married with her. But whether you can get out of here or not depends on you, not us."

I wanted to pay for her to stay in my home, where my sister, who spoke good English could help her. Her visa would expire in two months, and my family could help her while I was away. Of course, Chief Li refused.

On the 18th day inside Residential Surveillance, the fat policeman came and told me, "Your wife has already been deported back to Vietnam." When I heard this news, I was overcome with uncontrollable anger. Behind the anger was more sadness. I choked with tears.

When I was not being interrogated or forced to sit on the chair, I tried pacing around the cell to relieve my pressure and dispel my anger and sadness. I thought of [famous Chinese author] Lu Xun who spoke of writing a poem to express these kinds of feelings. I walked back and forth, back and forth, over and over, drafting and editing a poem in my mind. I have no talent for poetry, but it felt like the only way to record my sorrow. In the end, I faced the camera in my cell and wrote out the characters in the air for it to record my seven-line poem. Each time I wrote it out in front of the camera, I could feel a sense of revenge. I was sure they were watching and could see what I was writing.

After some three weeks or so I was taken from my cell and transferred from the Baiyun District Police Training Center to the Guangzhou Public Security Police Training Center. The new prison, despite its name, was not a training center. It was a Black Jail, transformed from an abandoned older police training center. The new training center, which was actually used as one, was nearby. During the latter part of my Residential Surveillance, while at this new facility, they would open the curtains sometimes, so I could see policemen filling up the facility and courtyards.

A stainless-steel gate guarded the compound, with armed officers standing by. Not even a bird could fly in [unnoticed]. Surveillance cameras covered both the outside and inside. Other people taken in Guangzhou during the Jasmine Revolution crackdown speak of being held here as well. My cell was slightly bigger, with steel bars as thick as fingers outside the window. This cell had two cameras. There were also two beds for the guards, instead of one. As before, the guards would work in shifts. At least two guards [watched over me] at the same time, sometimes up to four. Observing their routines, I quickly realized how difficult it would be to escape a Black Jail.

After a month of torture and maltreatment I lost my faith in the idea of the law in China. Earlier, I had often thought of the law as a life-saving straw; later, the very mention of the law mocked me. Political suppression is political suppression. It has no relationship with the law, a vacuum where all laws, all rights, are rejected.

The police had tried to make me write a statement to relinquish my rights to hire a lawyer, but I had refused. Later on, the police started "taking care" of my family. They would mention them in a threatening way. I felt so sorry for causing my family to be threatened because of my situation. I didn't want them to have to suffer or get into trouble.

In the end, I wrote the statement. And just as the police had said earlier, no lawyers would be allowed to get involved in my case at all. [Rights defense lawyer] Tang Jingling had been taken, and lawyer Liu Zhengqing had tried to become his lawyer. In the end, lawyer Liu was taken too, and both ended up facing charges of inciting the subversion of state power.

[Dissident artist] Ai Weiwei had been taken, the police told me. It had been a month or more when police suddenly told me. I had met with Ai Weiwei in Beijing, and had once been out to dinner with him and lawyer Li Heping. I answered calmly, "How is this related to me?" They said they didn't say there was any relationship. They just wanted to let me know and that I should give up dreaming. "No matter who you are, if you go against the Party, you can be taken."

There were new rules now. By this time, Pre-Trial Liang had taken over my case, and the guards were stricter. I had to ask for permission for everything: to use the toilet, drink water, etc. Without permission, I couldn't leave my seat or walk around. If there was no interrogation, I had to sit on a hard stool and reflect on my faults throughout the whole morning, afternoon, and evening. Pre-Trial Liang told me the Domestic Security Police had been too "easy" on me. The stool I had to sit on all day and evening was a wooden square stool, very thin. I started getting blisters on my butt, which started to bleed. It would hurt even more when I was allowed to shower. I tried to sit on the bed a little but the guards would start shouting and force me back to the wooden stool.

The combination of physical pain and mental anguish kept intensifying. My heart would pound and it was very uncomfortable. Some nights I needed to get out of bed and pace around because I felt so bad, but I was not allowed, and they forced me to lie back down.

During the first few months, I would scribble down some notes on paper when the police weren't there or were busy with something, and put them in an empty drawer next to the bed. Even the faintest ink was better than just a memory; I needed to prepare for my defense in court. I wrote in shorthand so that other people would not be able to understand. After two months, the paper I had was completely filled.

One day, an assistant of Pre-Trial Liang's suddenly rushed into the room and asked me what I was writing. He took out the paper filled with my shorthand notes from the drawer. I told him that they were my personal belongings and he had no right to confiscate them. He took them and left.

One morning, after more than two months had passed, I was sitting on the square wooden stool, when suddenly I heard someone speaking with a Hunan accent. "Is this Tang Jingling's room? I am the lawyer appointed by his family. I am here to meet him." I recognized the voice of lawyer Liu Zhengqing. The door of my cell was pushed open and lawyer Liu came in. I thought, the guards were so strict, how could he possibly get in? He started talking right away. "I'm here to meet Tang Jingling. I thought this was his room. You should sign a power of attorney right now. I can provide you with one." I didn't care about the prohibition about not hiring a lawyer. I immediately signed my name on the piece of paper he gave me. As soon as I had signed, Liu hurriedly left the room to look for Tang Jingling. I was very worried about whether he would be able to get out of this place. He might not know just how ruthless they were.

A few minutes later Chief Li came into my cell, brimming with rage, "What did Liu Zhengqing talk with you about? You said you would not appoint a lawyer, didn't you?" I responded that, "I didn't say anything. And you forced me not to appoint a lawyer, right?"

The police told me later that Liu was stupid enough to get in their way, so they had to keep him there. Just like that, Liu too became another inmate in this "prison." Liu would be stuck here for a month before being released on "bail."

One day, I was being interrogated by Mr. Tall, Rich, and Handsome when I suddenly felt waves in my stomach. I had to go to the toilet immediately, or else I would soil myself. Those days I often got diarrhea. I intentionally made it sound as bad as possible, and complained afterwards. "The meat is stinky. The fish is stinky. The tofu is stinky. The vegetables are stinky. How is it possible that I don't get diarrhea?" Mr. Tall, Rich and Handsome said he would report the problem. The food quality did improve after that.

After two months of harsh treatment, my case moved into a gentler period. Chief Li would come in for "chats." Obviously, this was fake kindness, bestowed after the previous suffering. He wanted to explain how I could move on. If I cooperated, I could restart my lawyer career, or start a new business. Nothing was a problem, only my attitude. I wanted to restart my lawyer career, but would never do so if I had to agree on some prerequisites.

If I had to go against my conscience, I'd rather not be a lawyer anymore. He listened to my answer then left looking resentful.

About three months into my Residential Surveillance, the Ningxia officer asked, "What are you going to do after you get out? Won't you continue your anti-Party work?" I knew that if I told them I would run a small business they would think I wouldn't have any time to worry about whether the Party was autocratic or not. I told him I wanted to continue as a lawyer but they wouldn't let me, so I would to start some kind of business. "What kind of business?" he asked. A buckwheat noodle restaurant, I answered. That wasn't enough; I had to write down a detailed business plan. Where was I going to open it? How much money would I invest in it? How would I attract customers? "We will only let you out if we believe that you really will do this," he said. So, I wrote a "business plan."

During my last period in Residential Surveillance, Pre-Trial Liang asked me, "Do you know what the spirit of Chinese law is? How would you summarize it in three words?" I answered, "Based on fact." No, he said.

"Law as criteria," I said. No, he said and shook his head.

I continued to look for three word expressions. "Rule under law?" A disdainful stare followed.

"Communist Party dictatorship," he said.

After hearing his answer, I felt like I had had an epiphany. He was absolutely right. The Constitution even talks about "the dictatorship of the Communist Party." All the "national security" crimes under the law are about protecting the one-Party dictatorship, nothing else. The law even prescribes that lawyers who are deemed to have gone against the Community Party's leadership and "socialist system" should be prohibited from practicing law. Even under civil and commercial law, the least political aspect of the law still has some element related to the one-Party dictatorship, even company law!

Inside Residential Surveillance, I wrote letters in which I made promises. I wrote apologies. I wrote what they wanted after all the torture. But one thing I never gave up was the attack on the street by the Domestic Security Police that started this whole experience. I refused to give up this claim.

A group of Domestic Security officers berated me and quibbled about it. They tried to make me change my mind, but I refused. One day, Smiling Tiger said; "I asked around about you being beaten. Nobody did it. After the Sun Zhigang incident [a migrant worker found beaten to death in police custody in 2003], Guangzhou police haven't beaten anyone. It might have been done by some other Domestic Security Police not under the Guangzhou police force."

So, he meant that I was beaten by police from a department lower down than the Guangzhou Public Security Bureau. Although I didn't completely believe him, at least he admitted, indirectly, one very important point: I had been beaten following an official order.

Later on, while Mr. Tall, Rich and Handsome was joking around with me, he leaked a secret too. One day I mentioned that I had lots of personal data on my computer, things that were private. He asked what kinds of things and I told him photos and videos of me with my wife. "Then I definitely want to have a look," he said with an exaggerated smile. I changed my mind, "Oh! I remembered wrong. It's not on the laptop." "Then where?" he asked, "The USB? The MP3?" No, I told him. "Then it must be in your camera, I am going to check it".

The camera, unlike all the other things, had not been taken in the raid on my home, but during the attack on the street! And they had it.

After my release, the pain in my left ribcage lasted for nearly six months. I could only sleep on the other side. While I was inside, the stiches on my leg had healed, but my ribs were still bad. Every time I spoke out loud or coughed, I'd feel pain. Towards the end, during a doctor's visit, I pointed this out, but before I had even finished my words, he had hurriedly turned around and left the cell.

Before they would release me, I had to forgo any claims to my house, which was technically owned by a collective. I also had to leave Guangzhou, and my release would be a "release on bail." At first, I didn't agree. I had bought that home in 2010, after losing my lawyer's license. I had had to sell my lawyer's office then, which I also used as a home, and this is what I had bought instead. But the police maintained a tough stance; telling me to not think I could be released without losing my home. They obviously wanted me out of the city. My desire for freedom won. It wasn't worth ending up in prison over a house. I accepted the humiliating condition.

After being inside Residential Surveillance for over 100 days, I returned home to pack. The door had been replaced; inside it was filled with spider webs, the place messy. More than anything, I looked around and realized my wife wasn't there anymore. I lost control of the tears that flowed from my eyes. The officer from Xinjiang saw my tears and stepped out of the room.

I had lived in Guangzhou for 11 years. All my possessions and memories of my life were in this house. [The officers I named] Dumpy and Xinjiang gave me two hours to pack what I needed. I had to abandon most of my stuff, amongst them case files covering 10 years of work.

On 12 June, I was released on bail. A total of four officers took me back to my hometown, in faraway Inner Mongolia. Once I arrived, I opened my laptop, and found all my personal data and information, spanning 10 years, had all been deleted. They had even swapped my hard drive to a smaller one! That data was priceless to me, and now it was all gone.

I tried to contact the number they left me, but the number was off all the time.

Although the Jasmine Revolution and my Residential Surveillance experience is already more than six years old, thinking back on my time inside and the torture still fills me with a lingering fear.

The system of Residential Surveillance at a Designated Location (RSDL) is actually a system of purgatory, created for prisoners of conscience. The purpose is simply to destroy you; to break you using any form of torture they want or feel is needed. Even more, it is used to make people in the community doubt each other, to make you incriminate not only yourself, but also others, to break the community. Even murderers don't have to go through RSDL!

During the Jasmine Revolution back in 2011, the authorities tested Residential Surveillance on a larger scale for the first time. They must have found it to be really valuable, and institutionalized it as RSDL in the revised Criminal Procedure Law the very next year. The new system was put into full effect starting in 2015 with the "709 Crackdown," or "war on lawyers." They expanded its use again in 2016.

By now, police are familiar and comfortable with using this new and powerful tool.

Chapter 3
My endless nightmare | **WANG YU**

Wang Yu (王宇), female, born 1971 in Inner Mongolia, is one of China's most respected human rights lawyers. Originally a commercial lawyer, Wang dedicated herself to rights defense work in 2011 after her own experiences with police abuse and wrongful imprisonment. She has represented ordinary citizens, Falun Gong practitioners, and feminists. Her most high-profile cases include defending Uyghur scholar Ilham Tohti, who was sentenced to life in prison in 2014 as punishment for encouraging ethnic unity, and Cao Shunli, a women's rights defender, who died in police custody the same year.

Wang's courageous rights defense work has won her several international human rights awards and nominations. But it has also meant that she is a frequent target of state repression. In the middle of the night, on 9 July 2015, the authorities abducted Wang from her home in Beijing. Her sudden disappearance sparked what would later be called the "709 Crackdown" when hundreds of rights lawyers and activists from across the country were secretly detained. Wang was finally released in August 2016. She was awarded the American Bar Association International Human Rights Award while she was in state custody.

"Hurting others is a kind of pleasure."
– Victor Hugo, *The Man who Laughs*

I will always treat 709 as my nightmare. In fact, it still haunts me. Many nights, even when I wake up from the nightmare, in reality I still feel trapped in it. I never imagined that human nature could be so evil, especially when I think of the young girls assigned to monitor me. I absolutely don't understand how these girls can face their lives in the future. I always felt that during my experience, those who suffered the most were not actually the detainees like me, but the girls assigned to monitor us.

It was 8 July 2015, shortly after 11pm. I had just said goodbye to my son [Bao Zhuoxuan], who was heading to Australia to study, and my husband [Bao Longjun, Chapter 11], who was accompanying him. Initially I had planned to go with them to the airport, but since the flight was at midnight my husband worried about me returning home alone. We decided I would say goodbye at the house. After they had left, I called to ask them to phone again after they had passed immigration. I couldn't control my sadness and cried on the phone. Even though I was trying to comfort my 16-year-old son, I was the one choking. My husband couldn't bear to hear our parting words and so he hung up. After the brief call, I went upstairs to prepare for a trial the following day. Later, after having changed into my pajamas and gotten into bed, I still couldn't stop thinking about Bao Zhuoxuan. I couldn't fall asleep.

It was after 1am and I still hadn't received a call saying that they had passed immigration. I tried reaching them but neither of their phones connected. At first, I thought it was because they didn't have a signal, but I had called many times, up to and after their scheduled takeoff time, and it was the same. I was growing worried. I sent some messages to friends in WeChat and Telegram groups, hoping they could help with some ideas. I called the airline, but couldn't get through.

Without warning, the lights in my house were cut, along with the internet, and immediately I heard the sound of someone trying to force open the door. Frantically, I sent out a message on social media, and everyone expressed their deep concern. One person replied asking if my lock was strong. I said it was, that Bao Longjun had changed it recently, and selected the strongest available lock, worrying that I wasn't safe alone at home. Another person replied suggesting that I put an obstacle in front of the door but I thought this wasn't necessary. If they could get through the door, then any obstacle would be useless. However, thinking back, if I could have put an obstacle between them and me, then it might have delayed them entering the room, and given me more time to spread the information of my abduction on social media, or to contact trusted friends and alert them directly.

I walked to the door, demanding, who is it? The sound of forced entry stopped as suddenly as it had begun. There were no more noises for a while. I sent another message to the groups, telling them that whoever it was must have left. Maybe they had just wanted to scare me. This type of situation had happened to a friend of mine before; they had just come to harass and intimidate him. I told the people in the chat group to just go to sleep. It was already 3am. I was still worried that I hadn't heard anything from my son and husband, and couldn't sleep, so I continued trying to reach the airlines, but nobody answered.

An hour later, at around 4am, I was shocked by a piercing noise. It sounded like they were trying to force open the door with an electric drill. I shared this message to the Telegram group immediately, and jumped out of bed. I tried to phone for help, but before anyone could answer, someone had already broken through the door, and was instantly upon me. The light from his headlamp flashed into my face as he spoke, "Don't move! We're from Beijing Public Security Bureau."

It had only taken a few seconds from the moment I heard the drill before they were inside.

"Who are you? How dare you break in? Show me your identification," I demanded.

I hadn't even finished speaking before more than a dozen people were inside, pushing me onto the bed, handcuffing me with my hands behind my back. In almost the same movement, someone was forcing a black hood over my head. He had a Tianjin accent.

Since I had already been illegally detained several times in the past by Public Security or court police during certain cases—you can imagine how much risk a lawyer with legal professional ethics faces in China—I wasn't immediately too scared. I tried to struggle, but it was impossible to make any difference as a woman against such a large number of attackers.

Two women in the group dragged me out. I tried getting the neighbor's attention, shouting loudly: "Don't drag me. I can walk by myself!" After they had dragged me into the elevator, I started crying. I asked them to release my handcuffs, saying they hurt my elbows. I knew there was a camera in the elevator, and hoped my lawyer might later be able to get the video record of that day.

They dragged me downstairs and threw me into a van. From what I could see from under the hood, there was a person in the seat in front of me. He looked like a boss. I sat behind the driver, two women on either side of me. Another three or four sat behind me.

Soon, I heard the vehicle in front of us starting to move; we pulled out of the housing unit, and I heard a few more cars following behind.

I cried the whole way, repeating what I had said in the elevator. The handcuffs were too tight. I repeated that they were supposed to show me their identification. A woman behind me, growing irritated, told me to shut up. But as she spoke, I detected a sense of fear in her voice, as if she was even more nervous than I was. I replied that if she were bound in tight handcuffs, then she would also feel pain. She had a bad temper. Suddenly, she reached from behind me, pressed down on my head, and tried putting a gag in my mouth. But I shut my mouth tightly. Maybe because the car was moving and she didn't have a good enough position to push me from behind, she gave up.

Afterward, I could feel that my hood was even tighter. I shouted: "I am suffocating. Someone give me some air!" A woman beside me adjusted my hood a little, and I could see a sliver of sky out of the side. The sky was just getting light.

I could see from the side of the hood that the van was entering Beijing No. 1 Detention Center, a familiar gate as I had often met clients there. I assumed this was where they were going to hold me. Not long after we entered, the car stopped. They told me to get out and stand beside it. One man undid my handcuffs and changed me into another pair that was not as tight. About 10 minutes later, they put me back inside the car. I realized that they weren't going to hold me at the detention center, but then where were we going?

We drove for about another hour. I could see from the gap in the hood that we were entering another gate, this one with armed soldiers outside. They even wore army helmets. They must have realized something was wrong, as they adjusted my hood again and I was plunged back into darkness.

After I was out of the car, they handed me over to two girls who dragged me by my sides. They led me up some steps: up, left, right, lift your feet etc. They seemed well trained.

After we arrived in a room, they took off my black hood and handcuffs. The two girls who had led me upstairs were wearing white T-shirts and black sweatpants. They were very young, about 20 years old. I observed the room. It was quite big. I assumed maybe 100sqm, like a small conference room. There were three big windows, but they were covered with heavy curtains so that you couldn't see if it was day or night outside.

There was a single bed on the opposite corner from the door, with folded bed sheets and a pillow. There was a desk, 4-5m from the bed, a red padded armchair, and four or five cameras on each section of the wall. Other than this, the room appeared empty.

I walked directly to the chair and sat down, leaning my head back. I told them I was too tired, that I hadn't slept the whole night and needed to rest. The two young girls told me this wasn't allowed. "Why?" I asked. "According to what regulation?"

At this moment, a short man in his 40s came into the room along with another two girls dressed the same. He ordered them to remove me from the chair, and then threw it across the room harshly. Foul-mouthed, he told them to change it for a square wooden stool, saying that was all I deserved. He promptly left the room.

Another girl came in. Pointing to the clothes on the table, she instructed me to change. I was still wearing my pajamas. My situation did not look good.

I requested to change in the privacy of the restroom, but they refused. I changed by half hiding behind the table and stool. It was very embarrassing. They made me wear a grey T-shirt and sweatpants.

As soon as I had changed my clothes, two men came in. The one in front looked about 40 years old, short, kind of fat, light skinned; he looked arrogant. The one behind him was older and taller. Wickedness emanated from his soul.

Once they were inside, the short guy said loudly with a strong Beijing accent, "Lawyer Wang, how is it going? Let's have a talk." I glanced at them contemptuously: "Who are you? What could I say to you? Let me go home!"

There was a camera on the wall directed at me.

After I had sat down, the short guy asked me to continue but I responded that he still hadn't told me who he was. He said his family name is Wang. "You can call me Chief Wang." I responded that my family name is also Wang. "Why are you Chief Wang?" The other man reprimanded me, "This is our Chief!" Turning to him, I asked which bureau he was from, and what was his name. Things went on like this. I kept asking them to show me their identification, to tell me their names, positions, bureaus, but I never knew their identities. I only learnt that one of them was called Chief Wang, and that they said they were from Beijing Public Security Criminal Investigation Unit Second Bureau.

Someone knocked on the door and came in with four boxes of food and a glass of water. Chief Wang made a sign to leave the food and let me eat. I hadn't slept all night, and didn't feel like eating but I wondered what kind of food it was. I opened the box: there were rice porridge, four buns and an egg inside, and four other kinds of dishes. I only ate one egg and some porridge. I drank some water, with a label marked "302" on the cup. This must have been my room number.

I asked Chief Wang what I could possibly speak with them about. As a lawyer, I respect and follow the law. "I have nothing to talk about with your kind of people, who casually kidnap others from their houses, without even showing a detention notice. Don't you feel ashamed to be police?" He lied to my face and said that they had given me the notice but that I had torn it up, when in fact I had never seen any such paper from them and nobody had identified themselves.

Chief Wang asked me to talk about how I entered this circle [the human rights lawyer community]. I told them that I was a lawyer. My work was independent, and I wasn't part of any so-called circle.

I was exhausted. I told them I needed to rest. I tried putting my head down on the table, but Chief Wang slammed the surface to keep me awake. I couldn't sleep.

During the whole morning, I refused to answer any of their questions. Even when they just asked my name, I didn't say anything.

At around noon, a girl came in with lunch. Chief Wang didn't see much progress and left. He handed me a notice before leaving. I was accused of "disturbing public order."

The food was not good.

After the meal, the man who had thrown the chair across the room when I had first arrived returned. He explained I would have to ask for permission to do anything. I demanded, "Which law says that?"

"Once you are here, you will follow the rules here."

I told him that I was exhausted, and needed to rest. He pointed to the bed. "Rest there," he said and left angrily. I fell asleep immediately. When someone woke me up, the room was filled with what looked like doctors and nurses in white coats. They measured my height, weight, blood pressure, body temperature, and asked about my medical history. I told them that my wrist was swollen from the handcuffs, and asked if they could give me some medicine. But they just looked at it and coldly turned away.

After the exam, another two girls came in, put me in handcuffs and a black hood, and took me downstairs into a car. I didn't know where they were going to take me.

The car stopped after only two minutes. We hadn't even gotten out of the yard. They took me to a room. Someone said they were going to take X-rays. I was still in the black hood and wearing handcuffs.

We went back to the car, this time it moved for less than a minute before they took me out. Again, I was transferred into the custody of another two girls. We turned several times before entering

The People's Republic of the Disappeared

a room. It was like an isolated monster's den, inside a small room on the gloomy side of the severely guarded courtyard.

This hidden location was where I would stay for the next month. Besides the roughly 20 girls who took turns monitoring me, and a few interrogators, I never saw another person.

They removed my black hood and handcuffs. I could see that we were in a cell built according to standard detention center layout. There was a long corridor, on the other side, a door, outside of which was the so-called exercise yard. Inside the room, on the right side, there were ten single beds close to each other, with a table beside the first bed. Bed sheets and pillows were stacked on several of the mattresses. There were two small plastic stools by one side. On the floor, a 40x40cm square was painted in red, and beside it another line painted in yellow; squares and lines presumably for controlling movement. A large sheet of glass separated the corridor from the bathroom, with a gap between for coming and going, but everything inside was clearly visible. There was a toilet, a sink, and a pipe with no nozzle for the shower. Three cameras lined the wall, with another camera in the bathroom. Later, I saw the label "207" written on a cup. I assumed that was my room number.

I asked if we were in a detention center and was there anyone else here. The room was so big for just one person, such a waste. They replied that I was the only one.

I was only allowed to sit in the square framed line they had painted on the floor. I wasn't allowed to make any movement outside the red and yellow lines; otherwise the armed police had the right to take any action against me. Again, I was told I needed to ask for permission before doing anything.

Another girl came in and told me to remove all my clothes. She claimed it was a routine inspection. I pointed out that that morning they had provided the clothes I was now wearing, I had just arrived, and had been surrounded by their people the whole time. "What could you possibly want to check?" Looking at the mounted cameras in the room, I said we should at least go into the bathroom; otherwise it was just intentionally insulting me.

She said no.

I was told to take off all my clothes, stand in the middle of the room for inspection, and to turn my body three times. I strongly objected to this insulting order. But these young girls didn't care.

They rushed forward, pushed me against the floor, and stripped me. I was crying, and pleading with them at the same time. Why would they insult me like this? Why didn't they have any compassion? Why were they so violent to a weak woman like me?

Perhaps I am a very traditional woman. I think the violent stripping off of my clothes was the biggest insult and torture I endured.

I demanded to speak with their superiors, to address this violent insult. At first, I was ignored completely. Later on, a man came in; he looked brutal and tough. He introduced himself as the team leader in charge of the facility. I told him what I had just gone through, that the action they had taken was illegal, that there were rules about it in detention center regulations, that it clearly violated my rights, and that I wanted to issue a complaint with the procuratorate. As I spoke, he was observably angry. He left without saying anything or letting me finish what I had to say.

Moments later, he returned with an even meaner looking man following behind him. He looked like a monster, with big eyes that shined with a brutal and evil light, a dark face, and crew cut hair. He was holding shackles in his hand.

The team leader gave the order, "Put them on her!" That monster grabbed my hands and feet, and handcuffed and shackled me. The handcuffs were not the normal type, but designed specifically for torture, made of pure pig iron, with tough 1cm thick rings.

My wrists became swollen after wearing them for a day, and even more than one year later my wrists still look a little black.

The shackles were also made from pure pig iron, the two rings even thicker, and in between them was a long chain with more than a dozen flat round links.

After putting me in handcuffs and shackles, the team leader left with these harsh parting words: "Didn't you want to meet the procuratorate? Don't you want to follow the law? This is it! If you don't behave well, we have something worse than this."

The shackles were very heavy. I almost couldn't walk as I was thin and weak. The two guards appeared shocked. It seemed that they had never seen this kind of situation before. It was hard to accept the reality of my situation. I had acted calmly; reasonably pointing out their illegal behavior, and in exchange, I got this kind of torture.

Besides thinking about the heavy handcuffs and shackles, I was still reflecting on the moment that they had stripped me, and I still hadn't slept properly. I felt dizzy; my stomach was brewing up a storm. I was going to vomit. I wanted to go to the bathroom, but I couldn't move. The two girls helped me. These two were the most compassionate of the many who took turns guarding me, but unfortunately, and perhaps because of their compassion, I never saw them again after that day.

While I was in the bathroom, vomiting, the two girls who had helped me were already being replaced with a new pair.

I was unaccustomed to the shackles. The new girls didn't help me. I returned to my place, inside the square frame painted on the floor. I sat there, with my stomach still in turmoil. I wanted to lie down to rest a little, but this was not allowed. I was very thirsty. I tried to take the water bottle in front of me, but one of girls quickly snatched it away, and put it on another table far from me. I told them that I wanted to have some water, but they ignored me. I tried to get up and get the water, but they blocked me, telling me that I couldn't move out of the square. I wasn't allowed beyond the red line.

Dinner came. I barely ate.

At 8 or 9 in the evening, two girls carried in an interrogation chair. The chair was coated in white steel plating, with a steel strap across the midsection. They placed the chair in between my square and the table and told me the interrogator was coming.

Chief Wang appeared with an interrogator. I call them interrogators, but they never officially told me that's what they were. I might otherwise call them police, but I had never seen them wear a uniform, and they never showed me any identification. For now allow me to call them interrogators.

When the interrogator saw my handcuffs and shackles, he gloated, and said happily, "Wow, wearing a bracelet, ha!"

Chief Wang pointed to the interrogation chair and said, "Lawyer Wang, take a seat." I glanced at the chair, replying, "I won't sit there. I am not a criminal. Why would I sit in an interrogation chair?"

Chief Wang looked at the two young girls and then at me, "Sit down. Don't embarrass me."

"I am telling you, I am not a criminal, and I won't sit," I persisted.

He rushed at me and, grabbing my right arm, threw me onto the chair and told the two girls to restrain me.

My right arm was in extreme pain. I almost teared up. I could see that my right arm was red and swollen. I held my tears and said nothing.

Chief Wang told me that I was being held on suspicion of "disturbing public order and inciting subversion of state power." Again, he asked me to address the charges. I looked at him, "I will never speak with someone who uses violence against me." I turned my face away and refused to talk.

A young man, not in uniform, walked in. He addressed me formally, "I am a police officer from Tianjin Public Security. My family name is Han." I didn't even look at him, which made him angry. He started attacking me, saying I was anti-socialist, anti-Communist Party, that I was a shrew [a common derogatory term for a nagging woman] etc. I didn't react; I just kept my eyes closed. They thought I was sleeping, so they shouted harshly and banged on the table and chair. Chief Wang forcefully smacked the back of my chair. It made me tremble from shock. But I remained silent and avoided eye contact.

I sat like this until the morning. They had been "educating" me, reprimanding me, but I never spoke a single word; I didn't even glance at them once. They were helpless. Finally, they called in the girls who were waiting outside, and left bitterly.

Once they had left, the two girls released me from the chair. I immediately fell onto the mattress, and was just about to sleep when they told me that I had to leave both hands outside of the covers when I slept. No sooner had I removed my hands from under the covers as per their instructions then they told me it was time to get up. I was so exhausted but I was helpless. I had no choice but to get up.

I understood clearly that they were intentionally making me suffer. I knew I couldn't do anything about it. I could only be strong, but I didn't know how many days I could hold out. I would just have to try, and when the time came when I couldn't, I would figure out a way.

It went on like that. I was forced to stay inside the small painted square during the day, suffering at the hands of these young girls. If my leg or a foot were out of the square, even by just a tiny bit, they would warn me or slap me. Sometimes they didn't allow me to drink anything at all, even if there was water in the room. I never had enough water. And after it got dark, the three interrogators would return, and initiate another kind of suffering.

After three days passed like this, the interrogators changed their attitude. They no longer insulted or admonished me; instead they poured me a bottle of warm water as soon as they arrived.

Then, during breakfast and lunch on the fourth day, after having just had a few bites of my food, the two young guards told me that mealtime was over. I tried explaining that I had just started eating. They repeated that mealtime was over. I quietly put down my chopsticks. I am not allowed to eat, I thought. Okay then! I won't eat. I would see what new tricks they were up to.

I was also considering another problem. Although they were all working together to hurt me, I was too weak to take them all on. I didn't have enough energy to argue with them about their illegal behavior. This place was absolutely isolated: any law, report, accusation, procuratorate were all so far away.

That evening, I couldn't stand it anymore. While they were still trying to persuade me to speak with them, I slowly felt my heart constrict, my breath became short, I felt dizzy. My body couldn't hold out any more. It was so painful I felt like I was going to die. My consciousness was slowly slipping away. My body fell from the chair. Even while I was weak and lying limply on the floor, they didn't plan to stop the torture. The interrogator dragged me back onto the chair. To prevent me from slipping out again, he restrained my chin and shackled my legs. They called in a woman who looked like a doctor. She opened my eyes, said I was okay, and then walked out.

At that point, Chief Wang said: "If you die here, you will just become another Cao Shunli."[1]

Indeed, I felt that I was dying. I had entered an empty state; a pain that is hard to describe. It was a feeling of exhaustion and depression. I couldn't breathe. I felt pain in every part of my body. I felt that my soul had already drifted away. That day, I thought, I really was like a dead person. I spent another sleepless night strapped in the chair.

On the fifth night, three interrogators came to speak with me again. They were still trying to persuade me to speak with them. They mentioned my son, but in a way that they were obviously holding back some information. I asked them harshly, "What have you done to my son? He is just a kid. It is too shameless of you to threaten me by using my son!"

"We didn't do anything to your son. He is good, just under our control. He didn't make it abroad, but that's okay. Once you get back, he can still go." Maybe because I am so close to him, I couldn't conceal my concern. This divulged a weakness for them to exploit. From that moment on, over the following year, they would often mention my son. When I did finally get back home after a year, I learned he had been under house arrest; that he had been prohibited from studying abroad; and had been monitored by more than a dozen guards every day.

He was so young. At just 16 years old, he had also become a victim of the regime. My heart was devastated. A regime that uses a mother's son to threaten her is shameless to the extreme.

It was around 4 or 5 in the morning, nearly dawn, when I fell unconsciousness again. I fell very unwell. There were countless golden sparks flashing in front of my eyes, every time I opened them. I saw the vague outline of three deformed interrogators. I felt that my life was fading away little by little. I couldn't stand it anymore.

I told them, I would talk, but I needed to have a rest first, otherwise I wouldn't be able to stay alive.

The People's Republic of the Disappeared

I would only talk about myself. I would not answer any questions about other people.

At that, they finally left, and allowed me to sleep.

On the morning of the sixth day, the three interrogators came back. They didn't wait until evening this time. Chief Wang looked very happy and smug. He told me, "I will ask them to undo your handcuffs so that you can have a good shower."

After that my daily schedule started to improve a little. I was almost permitted enough sleep. But since I hadn't slept at all for five days and nights, my sunken eyes and dark bags under my eyes never recovered. Even now my heart has problems.

Chief Wang went out for a while and then came back with the team leader and the "monster" to remove my handcuffs. The team leader pretended to look very sorry for me, like he was doing me such a big favor.

"Normally, in here, once we put handcuffs and shackles on someone, we keep them on for at least 15 days. Today Chief Wang asked us to remove them for you, so we will remove your handcuffs first, and only keep the shackles on you for two more days."

They took my handcuffs away. My wrists had become seriously swollen from the friction. If they hadn't taken them off, my hands would have been ruined.

When they removed my shackles on the seventh or eighth day, all of a sudden I felt my body was much lighter, just like the Chinese idiom, as light as a swallow.

Afterwards, when I reflect back on those days, I think perhaps God was protecting me. Somehow, I didn't get sick. Normally, I easily catch cold and have a weak body, but at that time my vitality and resistance were so strong. I must give thanks for the protection of God. When I reflect on Chief Wang's words, "If you die here, you will just become another Cao Shunli," it really makes me reflect on sister Cao's death.

During those days, Chief Wang also ridiculed me. "You worked so desperately for your clients before, but now, when you are in trouble, nobody cares about you."

I fought back with contempt. "Don't try to sow discord. It doesn't work with me."

Over the following 10 days, they interrogated me three times a day. The sessions would end only when the meal arrived, but the night interrogation lasted longer and later.

They began by asking about the cases I had represented, six in particular. They asked who had requested me to do the cases; how they had found me; who had introduced me; about the signing of the powers of attorney; and who had paid my lawyer's fee; etc. I replied that the cases they were asking about were definitely the more important cases I had done but that I had posted all the details on my Weibo and Wechat, and that they could get the information they wanted from those platforms. I explained that because my Weibo had been blocked, they would need special access. I pointed out that there was nothing illegal about those cases because I had already made them public.

They asked about my few trips abroad. They asked who had invited me; how they had contacted me; how I had traveled; who had bought my tickets; how many days I had been away; who had gone with me; and what kind of activities I had done there; etc.

They also asked about the workshops and gatherings I had attended a few times inside China. I told them that normally I was busy with my cases, although I participated a few times in a workshop or rights defense gathering, but not often. I was always busy, so I didn't have the brain capacity to remember these kinds of things.

Later on, they asked me to talk about my impressions of many people, such as [lawyers and activists] Zhou Shifeng, Wang Quanzhang, Liu Sixin, Wu Gan, Huang Liqun, Xie Yuandong, Li Heping, Xie Yanyi, Zhang Junjie, and Hu Guiyun. I told them I was a very typical feminist and didn't have much contact with these male lawyers, explaining that I didn't know them well and so I had no comment. In an attempt to sow discord, they often told me things such as: "Zhou Shifeng already said others use you like a gun. There is someone behind you. Zhou also said that you are stupid and will do any case."

They sometimes brought notes from Zhou Shifeng to show me, but I was not sure if they were real or not. Each time I told them he had the freedom to say what he wanted, but I only knew that I was a lawyer, so I would not allow others to tell me what to do. No one else has the right to tell me what to do. I take full responsibility for my own actions.

Toward the end of July, they tried persuading me to write a so-called confession letter and to deliver it on television. I refused without a second's thought. I would not write anything and would never go on their TV to confess.

After a few days, on maybe 4 or 5 August, Chief Wang came back. He took me into a room like a hotel, but obviously we hadn't left the yard. The room was decorated like a standard hotel room. There was a bathroom with a normal door. Towards the back was a table, in front of which was a blue armchair. There was a single bed. The room was not big, about 10sqm.

Chief Wang brought a camera with him this time. He still wanted me to reflect on my situation. I glared at him, saying nothing. I sat there the whole morning.

At around noon, Chief Wang disappointedly sent me back to the detention area.

On the morning of 7 August, the team leader took me to the so-called "Beijing Tongda Guesthouse." We could hear the sound of airplanes in the sky every day. In the beginning, I thought we were near one of the airports, but afterwards I learned from a base manager that it was the same location as my previous detention facility, on the edge of Beijing, inside a military base, in a small town in Hebei Province.

That day, Chief Wang came to tell me that the crime I was officially now suspected of was "inciting subversion of state power" and so they had changed my coercive measure to Residential Surveillance at a Designated Location.

I was speechless.

Later, one morning, Chief Wang showed up without any warning. He said that he had seen a post from my Weibo account that I had sent on the evening of 4 June 2013, to commemorate 6/4 [June 4, the Tiananmen Square Massacre]. He asked me what my purpose was.

I said I had had no purpose. It was just a commemoration. We went back and forth a few times. It was clear he really wanted to pin me down for saying something about 6/4.

Another time, they asked me about a dinner I had attended. Zhou Shifeng had invited some friends for a meal after the lawyers from the Jiansanjiang[2] case had returned to Beijing. They asked me if I had joined the meal. I explained that I went for meals so many times, how could I remember every single one? "What is the problem with eating together?" They wanted to know what Zhou Shifeng had said during the meal. I didn't remember. They said he had spoken against the Communist Party. I said I didn't hear any of that. I always went home early. I am a woman with a child; I would not take up too much time to go eating out.

This is what I had told them but when I checked the notes they had taken I could see they had written the opposite of what I had said. I pointed this out and requested that they change it. At first they refused, and, even worse, tried making me sign their libelous notes. If they didn't change it to what I had really said, I would not sign.

The Beijing interrogator started denouncing me angrily, saying, "We are treating you well these days. We changed your room. You have a place to walk around. We've been less strict with you. Now you are taking advantage of us!" I stared at him and spoke coldly, "No problem. You can send me back immediately." I turned my face away. The interrogator became anxious. He left the room. The interrogator from Tianjin stayed, saying, "He didn't mean anything bad. It was for your own good."

"If you are doing this for my own good, why not send me home?"

He said he would fix the notes.

The next day they took their revenge. After dinner, I was just about to shower, when the team leader came in with the "monster." The team leader spoke aggressively. "She didn't follow the rules. Change her chair!" The monster took the armchair away and swapped it for another iron stool. This one would be very painful to sit on.

I decided I would try to sit less, and do more activities on the floor. The iron stool needed to be moved several times a day to different places depending on whether I was sleeping, eating, resting or being interrogated. I considered it my exercise.

The interrogators were now playing "good cop." Every time they came, they would let me put a thick pad on top of the stool for support.

In September, they almost didn't come at all any more. Before, there were five teams of guards, with two-hour shifts. Now I had three teams per day, with three hours per shift. Those girls worked constantly. Their faces looked sallow.

On the afternoon of 8 September, Chief Wang appeared out of nowhere. He hadn't come for a long time. The Tianjin interrogator was with him. He said that there was good news. He would not be in charge of my case anymore. The Tianjin interrogator was taking over. He told me to get ready. They would come back to pick me up and take me to Tianjin. I thought, how is this good news?

After I had had dinner, the team leader came in and told me to be ready to go once he came back. He took out his gun and waved it around. I didn't know what he meant.

They put me in a black hood and two girls took me away from this so-called "Beijing Tongda Hostel" where I had lived for the past month. They handed me over to some Tianjin girls, who took me into a vehicle. We waited in the car for more than an hour. Then I heard many cars leaving one after another. After more than two hours, we arrived at the "Tianjin Jinan Hostel." What fate awaited me there?

Since being "released on bail," I have often wanted to write about my experiences. But so often, after picking up my pen, I found myself just putting it down again. I always felt that they were memories hard to look back upon, but that if I didn't record them in time, eventually they would fade away. So I forced myself to write this time.

I became stuck many times in the process and couldn't continue. I often had to stop and take a few deep breaths; otherwise I would become very depressed. It is a scar that has not healed for my family and I, even until today.

After I finished writing the story above, my spirits almost collapsed. Reliving these episodes was even harder than the moments I was actually there. I don't know why. While I was experiencing it, I didn't feel scared. Sometimes I had even adopted a "play" attitude in order to face it. It was almost fun to engage in a "battle of wits" with my captors and interrogators. But when I reflect back on these experiences now, it's hard, and I can't imagine how I was able to handle it. Sometimes, if I think about if it were to happen a second time, I ask myself would I be able to handle it again? Perhaps this is what is meant by "secondary trauma."

Chapter 4
Arise, ye who refuse to be slaves | **CHEN ZHIXIU**

Chen Zhixiu (陈志修), male, born 1979, is a human rights lawyer from Sichuan province who has represented some of China's most marginalized citizens. Along with investigating human rights violations and acting as legal counsel for rights defenders at risk, he has also researched and taught more effective ways to use the law in China.

In early 2016, the authorities placed Chen under Residential Surveillance at a Designated Location. Following his release on bail after a month, he was prohibited from leaving his hometown without police permission. The authorities have made it difficult for him to renew his lawyer's license, pressured the law firm where he was employed to fire him, and subjected him to additional surveillance to obstruct his rights work.

Chen Zhixiu is a pseudonym. Some of the details in his story have been changed to protect his identity out of concern for his safety. However, the account of his treatment by the authorities has been left unaltered.

It was early February, around 10am. I was preparing to leave to meet a friend for lunch when suddenly a group of people burst into my apartment. Somehow, it seems they had keys for the gate outside and for my front door. There were only three or four inside, but I could see many more lurking in the corridor and on the stairs, maybe a dozen in total. They must have been monitoring my computer and phone, as they seemed prepared for anything. Was there a bug in my room?

I would soon find out that they already knew my password and had accessed my normal email account but hadn't accessed or didn't know about my encrypted email. Maybe they had installed surveillance equipment in my house, and could see my computer screen. This seemed to prove that the government could monitor anyone, even those living in temporary rental accommodation.

I knew that the police had harassed my neighbors before I had left for a work trip out of China, and that they had also disturbed them while I was away. I later found out that while I was away the police had tricked my neighbors into going to the police station and had made copies of the house keys. This must be how they installed surveillance equipment when I was away but I had no idea their technology was so good. They must have seen all my emails and discussions about friends who had already disappeared into Residential Surveillance at a Designated Location (RSDL). It seemed hopeless, trying to second guess what they might know.

I was worried what they might do to me in order to force their way into my computer for the rest of the information they wanted. But at least I had already securely deleted a lot of sensitive case information from my hard drive so that they would be limited in what they could access after they took me. Still, I was trying frantically to remember what I had and hadn't managed to delete so I would be better prepared for the range of interrogations, and so I could do my best to protect others involved.

I had known they would eventually come for me. I couldn't escape this misfortune. They had "invited me for tea" [euphemism for a police summons] several times in the past few months. They asked about friends who were being held in secret detention. They had even kept me overnight in a police station a few weeks before. On that day, I had been planning to meet another lawyer, but before I could a Public Security Officer from Chengdu had unexpectedly called asking me to meet him. When I arrived, he was with Beijing Public Security officers. They kept me in the police station overnight. After they released me, I found out that another lawyer I knew had disappeared while I was in the police station. Things were getting serious.

After that night, Chengdu Public Security had come for me several times, accompanied by their Beijing counterparts. They had mainly asked about my relationship with a few key individuals in the rights defense community. I would tell them that I was just a lawyer hired by a small group of rights defenders to facilitate trainings for barefoot lawyers [unlicensed, often self-taught, rights lawyers]. The police had raided several of these training sessions so there was no point in me hiding my involvement with them.

After someone close to me disappeared, I had started to prepare for my own inevitable disappearance. I had arranged for my own lawyer in case I was taken, and set up an emergency contact. I left copies of my power of attorney at the offices of two lawyer friends and wrote letters to my parents and ex-girlfriend. I contacted a diplomat I knew and the Chinese Human Rights Lawyers Concern Group in Hong Kong, making sure they knew the lawyer I wanted to represent me if I was taken. At the same time, I had been destroying sensitive case documents, writing down questions to share with partners who had not yet been taken, and making a plan for how we would react to police interrogations. After that, I was just waiting for them to come.

Of course, several of my preemptive security efforts lost a degree of their value since it turned out that my computer and email were being monitored.

Somehow, I felt relaxed when they arrived, standing there in my small rented apartment. I was surrounded by threatening security agents and yet I was kind of happy. I had been so nervous over the previous days, unable to really concentrate on anything other than remembering to always look over my shoulder. I remember a friend had tried to convince me to escape from China, but I had no idea where to go, and so I had just been waiting. At least, when they burst into my apartment, I didn't have to be nervous about it anymore.

They moved quickly as soon as they broke into my place. They immediately confiscated my phone so that I would have no possible way to contact the outside world, no last second frantic call for help to alert the community, or delete any of my chat logs. Fortunately, I had already deleted photos and documents from my phone, so there wasn't anything for them to find but I hadn't deleted my social media apps before they arrived. They could see all the messages and group chats. I realized I should have been deleting messages regularly, setting chats to automatically self-destruct so as not to make trouble for others.

In the raid they searched everything, every corner, every piece of paper. They took out all my ID cards, bankcards, digital equipment, even my kindle and various useless chargers. They took everything. They told me to confirm what they were taking and to sign the confiscation notice. It was around noon by the time they were done.

They put a hood over my head and we left. Two people on either side of me walked me out of the door. I almost broke my ankle on the way outside because I couldn't see where I was walking. I could only overhear them on their walkie-talkies. They bundled me into a waiting car; it started to move. I had no idea where we were going.

I wasn't sure whether my neighbors had seen me being taken away but I had told them in advance to expect something and that they shouldn't worry. Knowing something would happen, I had asked one of them, a woman with whom I had a good relationship, to contact my ex-girlfriend so she could alert my lawyer. I had also asked that if any friends came around looking for me that she should tell them I had been taken so that the outside world would be sure to know what had happened.

The car stopped. They removed the hood from over my head and asked me to confirm that we were at my workplace. I was confused. It was the office of a civil society organization where I had once worked. They took me upstairs. A few of my former colleagues were there and I tried to give them a warning signal to not let on that they knew me. I wanted to protect them from also being taken in this crackdown. Nobody really seemed safe anymore.

They ordered me to point out the desk where I used to work and then asked if I still had any digital equipment there. An odd thing to assume, I thought. I explained that I had quit more than half a year earlier and hadn't left anything.

Afterwards, they covered my head again but right before they did I noticed that there were not just officers from State Security, there were also several from Public Security. As we drove away, I couldn't help but think how the authorities were using quite a lot of resources to detain me.

It took a long time to arrive at our destination, a length that was only compounded by the total darkness of having a hood covering my head. I couldn't see anything. All I knew was that we arrived in a parking lot and then I was taken up in an elevator, made to walk down a corridor into some room, and then confined to an interrogation chair.

I was made to wait for a long time. Nobody took off my hood but at one point I overheard someone on their walkie-talkie saying how someone else I knew had arrived. Would no one be spared? At least I had already done everything I could to prepare. I just hoped everyone else would react to the interrogation as we had discussed.

They had locked the board at the front of the interrogation chair, which pushed against my legs. I lost sense of time but I knew it was a long while. My head was still hooded but I focused on a tiny sliver of light from the direction of my chin.

When they finally came to remove the hood, it was suddenly dazzling, so many lights pointed towards me. I could see the place was well constructed. The walls were specially designed, padded for sound insulation and suicide prevention. There was an interrogation table, a big-screen television, speakers, a computer, and cameras in the room. There was a digital clock, displaying the date and time. I could see it was about 9pm. It had been almost 12 hours since they had stormed my apartment.

They gave me a medical examination. I told them that my heart and cervical vertebra were not so good. They tested my blood pressure.

They were about to do an EKG but skipped it because there wasn't a power supply.

They searched me. They took away everything I had with me. They even took away my belt, shoes and socks. I accepted that I was going to be interrogated barefoot. I had heard that these days were the coldest in 30 years. I could feel the chilliness of the floor. This was just the beginning; I would feel the same over the coming days.

I was being held on the first floor. That's why it was really cold.

The second morning after I was taken, the guard took off all my clothes, made me stand naked on the cold floor, and sing the national anthem [In September 2017 China passed a law making it a crime to disrespect the national anthem]. I asked them if the national anthem could only be sung while showing one's genitals. He didn't respond. I thought about the meaning of the line that says, "Stand up, ye who refuse to be slaves," and so I sang loudly, defiantly, and staring directly at them with anger.

"Arise, ye who refuse to be slaves!" I shouted. They stopped me and told me to get dressed.

I wasn't allowed to rest at all for the first three days. Even during the short breaks between interrogations, there were always two people watching me.

When they finally let me have some rest, I wasn't really allowed to sleep. They didn't allow me to wear any clothes to bed. The room was so cold, even though they had given me a blanket. I still couldn't handle that kind of cold. I was naked. A guard would come into my room and lift up the blanket to check if I was asleep. He pushed me around or hit my face, making excuses that it was to make sure I was still alive, and it was for my own good. I really wanted to swear at them. So even after they agreed to let me rest, I couldn't really sleep. This situation continued for more than 10 days.

The curtains were always drawn to block out the sunlight. They never opened them except once to let in some air.

For the first three days, my interrogations were continuous. There were always three interrogators. They would take turns, while the others rested. I wasn't given any rest or food. It wasn't until the third day that they gave me two small steamed buns and a few green vegetables. The size of the two buns together was still smaller than the palm of my hand. I felt that I was going to lose consciousness. I felt dizzy all the time because of the lack of food and sleep, but I was still expected to submit to being interrogated. If I started to wobble in the chair they would make horrifying sounds to snap me awake.

The interrogations were all very detailed. I had to answer their questions according to the plan I had made before but because my emails had been leaked and the deteriorating condition of my body and mind it became increasingly difficult. The information my interrogators provided seemed so detailed. I began to think that my resistance had been meaningless. They kept hammering on that what I was telling them was almost identical to what my partners had said, calling it part of our preemptive plan to lie. They accused me of being the mastermind, and of having planned how we would resist being questioned.

I wasn't worried about my treatment, because I didn't have time to worry. Whenever I wasn't facing off with my interrogators, I was thinking about the purpose of the interrogation, what they wanted to get from me, and what they already knew. I repeated my answers to myself, so that I could counter the next interrogation session and wouldn't make any mistakes or inconsistencies.

In the beginning, the interrogators focused on how I knew the other actors in the human rights movement. They wanted to know what kinds of things I was personally responsible for, where everyone lived, how I contacted them, and how we met up.

They didn't care so much about any training I had done abroad; instead they cared more about what we did inside China. After a few days, they were satisfied that I was just a legal trainer and didn't know about financing so they stopped asking me questions about foreign funding.

During the first three or four harsher days, my three interrogators acted out different roles. The main interrogator, I think his name was Yao, was often gentler than the others but he would still occasionally strike the table as a warning if he didn't like my answers.

The second one, let's call him Liao, was very tough, unfriendly and deceitful; he often yelled at me not to be shameless, saying he was giving me a chance to save face. Another one, a young fellow, I called Little Zhang, was impatient. It seemed he wanted me to cooperate with him mostly just so he could spend less time having to deal with me. They all took turns.

Yao would tell me that I shouldn't collaborate with foreigners because they were able leave at any time but I was Chinese and couldn't escape even if I wanted to. Liao would make things difficult for me when he was interrogating me alone. The young one, Little Zhang, struck me as kind of casual. He often told me to let him know if I needed any daily necessities, pretending to be my friend, as if I could believe any of my captors had my best interests at heart or that I would be tricked into divulging some secret because one interrogator smiled at me more than the others.

After a while, they changed the focus of their interrogation outside my immediate circle. They asked me about many human rights incidents that took place in recent years. They were specifically curious about the China Human Rights Lawyers Group.

They didn't think I was directly involved with many cases and I think they believed me when I denied supporting human rights work from behind the scenes. Before I was taken, but when I knew I was going to be detained, I had thought they would interrogate me about Wang Quanzhang, but in fact they didn't really ask me about him at all. He had only recently been formally charged after being held in secret for over six months and I knew several people who had been closely working with him but I convinced my interrogators that I had never worked directly with him, which in a way was true. They only asked me about Wang Quanzhang twice.

Throughout my interrogations, they used threats and psychological tactics. They would casually ask me if I thought my parents were healthy enough to survive my situation. They dug so deeply, the interrogators, to picture future outcomes and how that would impact my family. For example, if I was sentenced to 10 years, would my mother's health last that long? They mentioned examples of human rights workers whose families had died waiting for their loved ones to serve out their prison sentences. This approach made me extremely anxious.

I knew it was all threats and lies but their tactic worked. I did consider my parent's health. My mother's condition was already bad and I was honestly worried about whether she would be able to handle this. When the interrogators left me alone, my mind would wander to my parents. I wondered if they were already sick from learning about my disappearance or if they had gone to the hospital. I knew I couldn't do anything, but I couldn't stop myself from thinking about it. I have to admit, such psychological tactics worked well on me.

My interrogation sessions were filled with all manner of deception. They tried telling me that all my friends had already confessed, that they had put all the responsibility onto me. I didn't believe them, but by then I had been in their custody for several weeks and it was getting harder to resist. To convince me that my friends had sold me out, they showed me one confession letter they claimed was from one of my partners. They claimed that all my friends had already recorded video confessions and told me that I needed to do the same, that the video was for their superiors and if they were satisfied then I could be released. I agreed to be recorded, anything to put an end to my sleep deprivation and humiliation.

Since I had arrived, I hadn't been allowed to shower. It felt like my face and hair were full of oil. My nails were black. The first shower I had was because they wanted me to look clean for the video. I was allowed to brush my teeth and take a shower but I didn't have any clothes to change into. My clothes were never washed while I was inside. I could feel that my body had a peculiar smell but I kind of got used to it after a while.

It wasn't until a few days after the video was recorded that they threatened they were going to broadcast it on television. I remember arguing with them that they had lost all their credibility. Of course, I knew it wouldn't change anything.

The whole thing was so staged. First they brought me a draft that they had already written and asked me to copy it by hand. It made me feel a little bit like a schoolboy, copying whole books as if that was the way to learn. Despite the time they made me waste copying my confession, when we did start recording, someone stood behind the camera, holding up large note cards with my lines on them.

If I said something wrong, they made me repeat the line. My every word, the speed at which I spoke, my tone of voice, demeanor, everything had to be exactly right. If I said the wrong thing, we would do it over again. All in all, it took about seven hours.

After the long recording session, I felt very unwell. I hadn't eaten dinner. I am hypoglycemic and my blood sugar had gotten very low. I felt dizzy and sweaty. One of my guards actually seemed a little nervous, and he brought me some fruit and yogurt. After a while, I felt a bit better.

For a long time after I had made their video, they didn't interrogate me. I asked for something to read, a newspaper or a book, anything to pass the time. They refused.

Sometimes, I asked for a bottle of water. I would grip the bottle in my hands and stare at the label. At least it was something to read.

My daily routine had become to daydream and to reflect. I thought about a lot of things. I knew the confession video they made me do was a trick. After they threatened that it would be shown on television, I started to worry that if they did show it on television it could have a terrible effect on my reputation. How would they edit and use the video? I was worried people would think I had willingly denounced my friends and coworkers, given up easily. How would I explain myself, and even if I did explain would anyone believe me? Almost immediately, I feared the backlash of my forced confession.

The boredom was so bad that at times I would find myself counting the number of tiles in the floor or trying to eavesdrop on the guards' conversation. Once a guard played some Buddhist mantras on his phone. I was so happy to suddenly have something that took me away from the detention center. I became very aware of myself listening to and remembering the content of the mantras. Even after the guard went away, I was left thinking about the meaning of those

Buddhist words, and the irony of someone like that, in a place like this, listening to them.

One day, without any reasonable explanation, interrogator Yao suddenly came into my room. He ordered the guards to search me. They forced me to strip, checked my clothes, and made sure I wasn't hiding anything on my body. Then, without saying anything, they had me put my clothes back on. There was no explanation.

After the video confession, they started allowing me to shower, but the bathroom was covered with cameras monitoring me and I could hear the guards in the other room talking about me while they watched. The humiliation was constant.

My guards told me that my treatment was much better than the other "709" lawyers; at least I wasn't subjected to the "dangling chair" [See Xie Yang, Chapter 7] They may not have tortured me physically as they did the others, but in nearly a month of secret detention I wasn't really allowed to sleep at all. This was why my body was so weak after I was released.

In the last five days before they let me go, they started to interrogate me again, and frequently. They prepared some papers for me to sign, forcing my fingerprints onto my confession.

Before I was finally released, they asked me if I had a guarantor. I realized they were planning to release me on bail, a thought that hadn't previously crossed my mind. I gave them my parents' contact details. After some time, my parents and Chengdu State Security arrived to take me back. I was not allowed to return to Beijing.

Even after they released me from RSDL, I wasn't completely free. Beijing State Security continued to harass me. They would come to Chengdu every few months, sometimes with one of my interrogators. Each time they came, I can't describe how horrible I felt. I didn't want to meet them, or think about them, but I had to do as they ordered. Chengdu police did as their superiors in State Security commanded. Generally, they weren't too bad but for an entire year I was required to ask for their permission if I wanted to leave Chengdu for any reason. As a human rights lawyer who was used to taking cases around the country, this had the duel effect of cutting me off from my livelihood and closing another door of access to justice for victims who I might otherwise have defended or advised.

These are some of my memories from when the state disappeared me.

Chapter 5
Enhanced interrogation | **PETER DAHLIN**

Peter Dahlin, male, born 1980 in Sweden, moved to China in 2007 after working for the Swedish government. He first volunteered for the Empowerment and Rights Institute, an NGO founded by rights defender Hou Wenzhuo, who now lives in exile in Canada. In 2009, Dahlin, Michael Caster, and human rights lawyer Wang Quanzhang founded China Action, an NGO that provided legal and financial assistance to rights defenders at risk, trainings to develop the capacity of rights defense lawyers and local barefoot lawyers, and ran legal aid stations across China offering pro-bono legal help to victims of illegal government action from torture and arbitrary detention to land grabs.

Security agents detained Dahlin, his Chinese girlfriend, and several co-workers in early January 2016. They were placed under Residential Surveillance at a Designated Location in a secret custombuilt facility run by the Ministry of State Security in the outskirts of Beijing. After being made to appear in a nationally-televised forced confession, Dahlin was deported and banned from re-entering China.

They attached the electrodes to my fingers, one by one. They fixed two small cameras pointing directly at my pupils. A technician calibrated the machines that sat a short distance in front of me. Mr. Yang, played his usual role of "good cop," and so was a man I later learned might be called Mr. Liu, who played "bad cop."

Earlier in the day, Mr. Yang had entered my cell. I had been expecting another five to six hour interrogation session. Instead, he asked gently if I would like to partake in a "psychological test" aimed at "enhancing our communication." Eager for something new, I said fine. Afterwards, I was taken into the interrogation room across the hall from my cell. It didn't take long to realize that this so-called psychological test was in fact a lie detector test. As with the video "confession" they asked for a few days later, they had anticipated my cooperation, and everything had already been set up before I walked into the room.

As they were strapping the electrodes to my fingers, I sat there thinking about what had happened a few nights earlier. During one of my regular interrogation sessions, they had sprung a document on me. A surprise: an internal review document of our work with the National Endowment for Democracy (NED). Intended for NED board members only, this was the kind of document not even we, as a grantee, would have seen. A sloppy hand written translation into Chinese was attached to the document they showed me.

Until that point, I thought they had come around to believing I was being forthcoming with them. Although the NED document they presented didn't actually counter anything I had said earlier, it certainly added details to our work, details I had tried to avoid. Perhaps seeing it had woken them up, alerted them to the fact that I may have been holding back. They must have assumed a lie detector test could break through the barrier and get me to be more forthcoming. I had never heard of anyone else being given a lie detector test, although I later learned they did threaten my girlfriend with one.

It wasn't just me. Five people I had been working with had been taken in, over a few weeks, through the same operation, spanning several provinces. It was serious, although not entirely surprising. In fact, I had been expecting something. I had just been a little too slow.

For more than a week before I was taken, I had been scrubbing my phones and memory cards, making digital copies of documents and receipts, spending what felt like days on end hunched over the paper shredder. If I was going to be taken, I wanted to make sure any material lying around didn't incriminate me, provide evidence, or lead the police to staff or partners. I had a plan. Late at night, I snuck out of my small home in Beijing, with shredded papers stuffed in a sports bag, and wound my way through the labyrinth of small alleys, stopping at various trashcans where I scattered the shredded papers, making sure to evade the myriad of cameras that line the streets of Beijing.

I had booked a flight out of China to meet my parents, just another trip to Thailand as I had made many times before. In the last few days before the raid, as pressure was mounting, my girl, Jinling (Chapter 6), and I had decided to change the plan. This time, I would not be coming back to China.

Jinling would quit her job and prepare to join me outside China a month later. I had packed my bags, but started re-packing, distracted by the uncertainty of what to bring when fleeing a country I had lived in for almost a decade.

It had sounded like such a good plan, in my mind, but how it had unraveled, I thought as I was sitting there strapped into a tiger chair [a chair with ankle and wrist clamps, often used as a torture device] being prepped for a lie detector test. Until the moment the police arrived, I had thought I was one step ahead. I had thought I would be okay if I left China unexpectedly and had moved my scheduled flight to Thailand about 36 hours earlier than originally booked. But, as it turned out, they were well aware of my plans.

I was in bed with my girl, spending our last few hours together before I had to leave, when, at around 10 at night, we were startled by a sharp knock on the door.

I opened the door in my underwear, greeting the authorities and their assembled cameras with a faux sense of calm and surprise, boosted by the hope that the Xanax pill I had popped on my way to greet them would soon take effect. Working and living under the threat of detention, arrest, or imprisonment for many years had already taken its toll on my mental health. Severe anxiety had become a constant reminder of that reality and I had long since taken to keeping, but rarely using, Xanax when things got bad. But they had never gotten this bad.

The lie detector test was their last hope to puncture the story I had been repeating over the previous couple of weeks of interrogation. If they were going to force me to say more, they needed to find a lie, a contradiction, in my story. They failed.

The test went on for most of the evening. The questions themselves were largely the same that they had been asking me for weeks, coupled with control questions to test the machine. They asked what our NGO did. They asked about our relationship with the Feng Rui Law firm, which was at the center of the "war on lawyers" campaign. As always, they focused on Wang Quanzhang, the human rights lawyer and my old friend, as well as asking about Xing Qingxian, a barefoot lawyer from southwestern China and Su Changlan, a brave woman in southern China who had been organizing support activities in the mainland for Hong Kong's Occupy Central [pro-democracy] movement.

The sweat on my fingertips required many repeats and restarts. I told them that I sweat a lot when I am anxious. As always in interrogations, it became about parrying their attempts to misinterpret my answers to their advantage. In the end, the session did not seem to have yielded any success for them. They had failed at uncovering any contradictions in my testimony. I had defeated a lie detector test. I couldn't hold back the feeling that by extension I had defeated them. The test itself, my answers, and their interpretations of them were never mentioned again.

My first line of defense was never meant to last, that I was a trust-fund kid who occasionally did some work for the family business in China. They had enough evidence to know my actual work and my role in the NGO I had co-founded. There was a plan. With friends and partners having been through interrogations, kidnappings, detentions, and torture, I had learned plenty about how the state operates. Published accounts on interrogations had helped even more. There were red lines that couldn't be crossed, there were standard methods used, and knowledge of this was of great help. I had avidly read these accounts and often encouraged grassroots partners to do the same, to be prepared if they were ever detained. Of course, I am a foreigner, and not only that, a foreigner from a western country, and with a white face. I never assumed that physical torture would be part of anything they would use against me—unlike most of my Chinese friends and colleagues. I knew any treatment used against me would be mild in comparison to what Chinese activists would face.

Adding another layer of physical protection, the fact that I had a very rare, and dangerous, autoimmune disease, Addison's, actually played to my advantage for the first time. Because any extreme physical or mental stress could trigger an adrenal failure, leading to a coma or death, they knew they had to be cautious.

They didn't want a dead foreigner on their hands.

Why had they decided to take me when they did? State Security had attempted to plant a mole in our organization back in 2013. Provincial police and State Security had raided and shut down numerous activities we had organized over the years. Partners had been detained, interrogated, and my name had come up when they had questioned human rights lawyers or partners before. Some had even gone on to prison knowing my name and the name of our organization. So why had they come for me when they did?

Wang Quanzhang, a human rights lawyer, was the co-founder of the NGO I ran. My interrogators asked me a lot of questions about Wang. We had worked together as far back as 2008, and over the years we had collaborated with many of the lawyers taken in the "709 Crackdown." But Wang and I had professionally parted ways before the crackdown began, having largely stopped working together in 2014. Wang had been taken long before me, in August 2015. After I was released, I found out that during my time under Residential Surveillance at a Designated Location (RSDL), my old friend had been transferred out of his RSDL and into criminal detention but that hadn't ended his enforced disappearance. As I write this, Wang remains missing. He might not even be alive anymore.

Su Changlan had been in detention a long time by the time I was taken. It was true she had worked for us, as we had supported her to run a one-woman legal aid center, offering pro-bono legal counsel to victims. But our work together had ended before the Occupy Central Movement began, and we had no relationship with her concerning her work for that movement. But it didn't stop my interrogators from demanding information from me on Su Changlan and the democracy movement in Hong Kong.

A few months before I was taken, Xing Qingxian, along with Tang Zhishun (Chapter 9), had been detained in Myanmar trying to smuggle the son of lawyer Wang Yu (Chapter 3) out of the country, to Bangkok, Thailand, and onwards to the United States. Both had been in RSDL for months before I was taken. I hadn't even been in the country at the time, in October, returning only two days after they had been disappeared inside Myanmar. The situation didn't look good, obviously, but I wasn't even aware of the efforts to help Wang Yu's son escape. I had only read about it in the news like everyone else. It didn't' matter how many times I explained it. State Security was convinced that I was the mastermind behind the plan. Yes, my NGO had worked with Xing in the past but that had stopped some time earlier. Like Su Changlan, we had supported Xing to run a legal aid center. He was the only one of our extended local staff that I had communicated with directly, in breach of our security protocol, which usually saw several layers of communication between the core staff and our local partners. This was done to protect everyone involved, but had not been followed for Xing. Xing knew I was a foreigner, he knew my first name, and one of my email addresses. It was enough for the police to piece things together.

In the end, who told the police about me, and why, I don't know for sure, and frankly I don't care. Whoever it was had to take steps to protect themselves, and as a foreigner, I was in a far better position. But this hadn't stopped State Security from trying to convince me that everyone had tried to sell me out. They showed evidence that this or that person was blaming me. Pretending to have my best interests at heart, my interrogators told me I had to protect myself and denounce those who were blaming me, or else I would take the fall all by myself.

My "crime" had a minimum sentence of five years in prison, and with my medical condition, they made it clear, there was little chance of surviving. Which is true. The problem was they picked the wrong people to say I was being sold out, trying to make me play the blame game with individuals I consider the best people I have ever met. This is especially true of a man named "Xing," who appears with me in the CCTV-aired "confession" video they later made me record [a different Xing, not the Xing Qingxian caught in Myanmar]. Xing, a local farmer turned self-taught barefoot lawyer, is perhaps the most good-hearted man I've ever met. I have yet to meet a man who I respect as much as him, for his pure moral code. I could say nothing other than he and the others were the best China has to offer, and the government should be proud of them, not persecute them. I refused to sell them out, and my interrogators stopped trying.

As they say in politics, never lie about things people will find out about anyway. The fact that most of what I said was true also made my plan more effective. I kept at it, and spent my time painting a frame without much content. What was my role in the NGO? I was an administrator, never involved in any field activities, my white face and limited Chinese language skills made it impossible. I was just an administrator. Luckily, Michael Caster, the only other foreigner in the NGO, was out of the country and safe from any state reprisal. I used him. He was the one handling outreach, which was true. Questions about what journalists we knew, what diplomats we worked with, or other NGOs and rights defenders, that was all Michael's domain I explained. Of course, I also knew most of the journalists or diplomats we had communicated with in Beijing, but again I focused on portraying a fuzzy picture without detail.

Who are the Chinese staff? I said they were merely contractors. Documents they had might have shown them as staff, but in reality, I explained, we only paid them for specific work on individual projects. They couldn't possibly know much about the organization, as they were only involved in individual projects and activities. My frame was too wide and empty, while my coworker's information was far too detailed and specific about the smallest thing. Combining the two could not give the authorities a full picture.

They had a general idea of our income, but I had to make them believe that much of the money we received from our donors never entered China, that it wasn't used for fieldwork inside the country. I had to make them believe that our work was as little as possible, to diminish our impact, which was our perceived threat to the Party, to protect our staff. My idea worked by playing into the state's own propaganda against foreigners. I told them, Michael and I used the organization's savings for living a high life, keeping the money for ourselves. This accusation, that we were embezzling funds, would later become part of their smear campaign against the NGO and me, but it had come from me, to protect all our Chinese partners. Their limited understanding of strict policies on accounting, external audits, and the reality of international donor controls for the funds they provide made it an effective lie.

All in all, many local partners around the country never knew Michael or me. Even though Michael had actually visited many of our field activities over the years, he would sometimes use a pseudonym when introducing himself to barefoot lawyers or grassroots rights defenders and never identified the organization name behind whatever project or activity they were participating in. We attempted as much as possible to ensure that communication between field partners and those in Beijing went through intermediaries, in different cells around the country. Almost no one actually knew everyone else. Only two people ever knew about all of our activities, donors, staff and partners—Michael and I.

Despite cleaning most of the hard drives and USBs, and using encryption on work document storage, passwords to which they never got from me, they still got information. Almost every day, sometimes twice, they would walk in with some new printed material. Limited access to a coworker's email showed the instructions I had sent out on the day I was taken, instructions to destroy evidence. They would show me summaries of what they had gotten from others, to make me believe that people were talking voluntarily. Most threatening, however, was the use of file recovery programs. They would find and recover random documents, or parts of documents, from one of the hard drives they had confiscated from my apartment—some recent, some many years old. Every day had to be spent in preparation for what the next document they recovered might be. Basically, they could re-create documents that had been deleted long ago, or parts of them. Luckily most of what they got was not very useful, but the knowledge that the next day they could walk in with something, a budget, a project plan, a list of people, audit reports, or receipts, kept me on my toes.

Knowing new documents were forthcoming, along with the five to six hour-long interrogation sessions that often started in the evening, coupled with occasional sleep deprivation, made the whole process quite intense. It was a battle of intellects. I had to protect as much information as possible, while making sure never to directly lie, as the very next document could uncover any untruth. And if caught actually lying, everything would collapse. Looking back, it's hard to imagine that I managed to keep my brain alert enough to be able to spin my interrogators in circles, during those sessions every single brain cell was focused on this one task.

During the lulls in interrogation, I would carefully go over the experiences of the past few weeks, retracing forward and backward from the night they took me, and the days in between.

My experience in RSDL hadn't started too badly. The morning after they had taken me, when I woke up, a bag of cold KFC was waiting for me on a table inside my cell. It was allowed to sit in one of the two comfortable chairs in my cell. Maybe it wasn't going to be so bad after all, I thought to myself. Later that evening, after 24 hours had passed, I was told what was to come.

I was being placed in "Residential Surveillance at a Designated Location." I had a long list of rights read to me. These rights consisted of being allowed to ask for things, but not to get them. My suspected "crime" concerned national security. I had the right to ask for a lawyer, but I did not have the right to receive a lawyer. I had the right to meet Embassy personnel, but the authorities could make me wait as long as they wanted before allowing me to meet anyone from my Embassy.

The law says you can be placed in RSDL for a maximum of six months and in reality almost all instances last the full six months. At the time, there was no doubt in my mind. Of course, solitary confinement might not be the right word. The two comfortable chairs in my cell were usually taken up by teams of two guards. In six-hour shifts, 24 hours a day, they would sit there, staring at me, taking notes on any little thing, but not speaking.

After the first two or three days, the mind games in this suicide-padded cell would begin. Tactics straight from old US cop movies. They would cover the two windows with heavy curtains, blocking any and all light. Large intimidating groups would enter the room abruptly, surround me menacingly and then leave. Later they would put some tape over the thermometer reader by the door. I could never figure out the purpose of that.

By my first weekend, I heard sounds of slamming and screeching from the floor above that went on in regular intervals all night. There would be no sleep under these conditions. But they had already subjected me to sleep deprivation. Earlier, they had refused to let me sleep unless I wrote down some information for them. I had asked for the boss, and told her about China's ratification of the Convention Against Torture, arguing it defined sleep deprivation as a form of torture. She, an older woman, was fuming. Had I no respect? They were treating me so nicely, she yelled. In the end, rather than directly subject me to sleep deprivation, they would use slamming, screeching and loud noises from upstairs to keep me awake, to break me down.

During this time, the "bad cop" was intimidating and aggressive in an effort to try and get what he wanted. He was often shouting and getting angry. It was his way to get me to write down the "evidence" they wanted, but I refused, saying that I would not write anything until I had seen someone from my Embassy. After that, and the shouting match with the superior about sleep deprivation, the "bad cop" took a back seat, and the "good cop" handled most of the interrogations, trying a different tactic. I think there were about 10 days in a row when I didn't see any sunlight, just the fluorescent overhead lights that were on 24/7. They were always on, but during those days, the bulb right over the bed would be kept on as well, not just the bulbs in the other parts of the cell.

The worst of the treatment had ended by the time I was hooked up to the lie detector test.

Sitting there, another issue occupied my mind. Several years earlier, when I was living with my former girlfriend, I had been using my apartment as an office and she had also assisted with some minor translation work. In this way, she had met many of China's premier human rights lawyers and rights defenders. We had not only had a very long list of lawyers, journalists and rights defenders visiting the apartment for work but had also hosted many of them for social events. I introduced Wang Quanzhang to Scandinavian Christmas at our house, having him over for Christmas dinners twice and Xing, the farmer-turned-activist, had been introduced to Thanksgiving at our apartment. We had even let him cut the turkey. It was impossible the police didn't know of this place, and thus about my ex-girlfriend. We had remained friends after breaking up and so I knew she had been traveling out of the country when I was taken but I also knew she was scheduled to return, by my calculations that would be around the time of that lie detector test. I had become increasingly worried they would take her too. I spent many free moments trying to think if there was somehow a way to get a message to her, but of course it was futile. After I was released, I found out I had spent sleepless nights for nothing, she hadn't had any trouble.

At times they would move me out of my cell and put me in the tiger chair. I would hear a large group of people entering my cell, moving things around by the sound of it. Some 20 or 30 minutes later I would be taken back. Were they reorganizing my cell to make it look good for an Embassy visit? In the end, it turned out no. Were they doing the same for visits by the prosecutor, who is supposed to supervise those inside RSDL to make sure no torture is ongoing? I still have no answer what this was about. There was a TV cable outlet. Did they install a TV and nice chair, for the prosecutor's weekly oversight visit? Did the prosecutor even visit? I don't know. The month after my release, a new regulation came out stipulating that yes, weekly visits by the prosecutor's office are mandatory, to prevent abuse and torture, but of course, if police claim such a visit might hinder the investigation, they can refuse. In the end, the regulation is not worth the paper it's written on.

As the formal interrogation sessions dwindled after the first two weeks, Yang's visits to my cell in the afternoons or evenings increased. I thought of them as "fireside chats," cozy and informal talks, but without any actual fireplace of course. Philosophical discussions, informal talks. He would tell the guards to bring cigarettes and let me smoke. Bland Nescafe was given. He was working hard to find a good solution; he was on my side, he explained. He wanted me out, the better for both of us. This was another tactic to create a sense of dependency. With him visiting, the curtains could be pulled open, allowing sunlight in. I could smoke; have a coffee. They wanted me to look forward to his visits. One time, he told me he was going to court to argue my case. Even more surprisingly, he asked if I wanted him to pick up some meatballs for dinner at the IKEA store. We settled on him getting me a real coffee from Starbucks, and a sandwich. But I was less lucky when it came to other requests.

Books or things to read were never given. I was to suffer from a lack of distractions. I would spend the days trying to remember the lyrics to a lot of songs, especially Bob Dylan's *Love minus zero / no limit*. Anything to distract my mind; to avoid thinking about the same things over and over and over. Looking into the blue-grayish suicide padding, each minute would feel like an hour, part of the tactics of secret detention. After the interrogations dwindled, my treatment had improved, but life became harder. No stimulation other than our brief, occasional "fireside chats," fried my mind. At least when they were interrogating me there was something to break up the monotony. Each memory would be processed ten times over. Every romantic experience, every friendship, every Christmas, and more, was analyzed in my head over and over and over. Planning an escape became a recurring thought, but it was impossible. Thinking of suicide became a recurring thought too, but that was just as impossible. It was never a real consideration, but analyzing if it was even possible went on, and I would test scenarios in my head, but none of the ways I dreamt up would have worked. The cell, the guard rotation, the guard dogs in the courtyard outside, it was all too well set up. Even the toilet seat was padded. There was no way out. Even if I asked for some water, meaning one guard would leave temporarily to get it, or get lunch or dinner, which was eaten on my narrow bed, the remaining guard would hand his key to the other guard. There was no way out, neither through escape or suicide.

I had seen the occasional story in expat magazines about Dongcheng District Detention Center Number 2. It was the place foreigners were placed in pre-trial detention. It has a special wing for foreign inmates. Stories would range from depressing accounts of life inside to "feel good" stories about charitable organizations holding Christmas dinners and similar activities there. Six months in RSDL would, without a doubt, I thought, be followed by 12 to 18 months in pre-trial detention. Any diplomatic solution, I assumed, for example, medical parole, would be considered by the time of my trial but not before. I was in for the long game, I was sure. The idea of being allowed one hour outside for exercise, such as in a formal detention center, seemed like a dream compared to being cooped up in RSDL. Books could be borrowed and read. You could talk with other inmates. Could I somehow speed up the process of being moved, instead of wasting away in solitary confinement under RSDL? At this point I would have read the phone book had I had the option.

This daydream, and thoughts about longer-term placement in prison, became something to hang on to. Would I be allowed visitors in prison and would I see Jinling? I went over the same conversation with her over and over again, switching between telling her I desperately needed her visits to sustain me, to telling her that she needed to move on, to find a new man, that she couldn't waste her entire youth waiting maybe ten years for me to be released.

Contradictions. So many thoughts would come and go, and often contradict each other. While daydreaming about Jinling and life in prison, I would also be well aware that it was never going to happen.

I would be dead before then. My medical condition would see to that, no matter how much hospital care they might provide. It was a matter of when, not if. Could I last a year, maybe two? Strangely enough, it didn't worry me as much as I thought it would, maybe because it never seemed real.

Luckily, such recurring daydreams were interrupted when more interrogations were demanded. A formal deposition followed very late one night, after about two weeks of daily or nightly interrogations. It summarized all that had been said before. As always, they wanted to misinterpret my words. Placing words in my mouth. Wang Quanzhang should be called a criminal. It was a constant back and forth, and I refused. How can someone be a criminal if they have not been convicted of any criminal act? The next day Yang came back. My written, re-written and re-written again confession was not strong enough for the panel of judges to take a decision on my situation. Medical parole, for diplomatic reasons, was the best way forward. He needed my help. Let's record a video that we can show the judges, he said. I agreed.

The answers and questions had been prepared for me and written down. All I had to do was act it out, with an appropriate demeanor. Some lines were taken from a meme, such as, "I have hurt the feelings of the Chinese people." Once taken across the hall to the meeting room, next to the interrogation room, in the secure wing that was my area of the secret prison, it became clear that this was no recorded message for a panel of judges. It was theater for public propaganda. A CCTV "reporter" would play out the act with me. The making of the video took one evening, and the only point of contention was again calling certain people criminals. I refused. They eventually relented. I could also be vague on the point of criminal activities, and not directly say that my work activities had been criminal. Our work had operated without formal recognition, and no taxes had been paid, so it was technically true, that I had indeed broken the law. It would be a long time before I actually saw the video myself, but it didn't take long after my release to realize they had used it to scaremonger foreigners, foreign NGOs, and their supporters.

Not long after recording the "confession," I was told that I was to be allowed to see my girlfriend. It had always been made clear that her case would not get a resolution unless mine did. I became certain I was to be deported. The same day, or maybe the next day, I was taken to the interrogation room and told I was indeed going to be deported— be it in days, weeks or more, they couldn't say. My first tears appeared in my eyes as they told me Jinling would be released, and all her charges dropped. She would be free.

The next day we were allowed to meet in the same meeting room where they had made the forced confession. We had both been told to put on our regular clothing, just like I had for my earlier CCTV recording. Her hair was standing out in all directions, looking like a witch. Despite that, she had never looked more beautiful to me. The translator used a handheld camera to record the whole thing, with Liu, the "bad cop," monitoring. A hug was allowed, but not a kiss. Not that we paid attention. Liu had to tell us to stop kissing. After all this, was our plan still on? It had already been decided we would leave China, both of us, together. Being much stronger than I will ever be, she hadn't been swayed. Yes, our plan was still on. State Security's attempt to sway her had failed. Later I learned that they had told her that I had paid my ex-girlfriend to be my mistress; that I had children and a family outside of China; that I was a bad influence; and, she should think of her motherland. They had tried it all. The next 30 minutes was spent making practical arrangements. She would be allowed to pack a small bag of things from my house for me to take with me.

The interrogations of the first two weeks and later solitary monotony were too intense for me to let down my guard at the time.

It all unraveled in a hotel room in Copenhagen, when my brain finally allowed itself to wind down, and process what had happened to me. My deportation had been interesting, and the flight had had problems. It ended with an unplanned stop in Helsinki to change crew, and before arriving at Copenhagen to switch flights it was too late and we were put up in a hotel. That night, I didn't want to do anything but sleep, but it all started coming apart. It didn't end in Copenhagen.

For the next few months it got worse, step-by-step, with various symptoms. I would snap and get angry for nothing. I would feel trapped even just having conversations if I felt it was going on for too long, if it didn't get to the point fast enough. Standing in line in shops became intolerable, and panic attacks mounted in almost every situation where I felt I wasn't in complete control. Shaking and anxiety became part of life. Luckily, having worked to provide mental health support to rights defenders, and having many friends who had suffered post-traumatic stress disorder issues, I was able to identify what was going on, and in doing so eventually got a grip on the situation. I'd be lying if I said it's all been made to go away, but after maybe six months, it had become manageable at least, and most of it "solved."

When Jinling and I had met in that room for the first time in weeks, I had asked her repeatedly if our plan to move to Southeast Asia was still on and although she had kept reassuring me, with tears in her eyes that made me believe it, we had no way of knowing if she would actually be allowed to leave the country. It is true that State Security had told her they would not prevent her from leaving China, but there was no way to be sure, until she was off the flight and far from China. It would be more than a month before we could meet up, as I was sent back to Sweden, and had to spend some time recovering, and she had to return to her hometown to prepare to leave. In the end, they kept their word, and she was allowed to board a flight out of China.

Her departure was far less dramatic than my deportation. Much like when I was first taken, I was blindfolded and driven straight from the secret prison to the airport. Four intimidating men, all wearing what looked like martial arts gear, took me. I was not allowed to speak except in the case of a medical emergency. They must have been enforcers. They looked more intimidating than anyone I'd ever seen. Hitmen? Other officers and police followed, five cars in total. We entered from the backway, and I was taken to a reception area. More police and cameras appeared as my deportation order was read out. I was to be deported under the Espionage Law. I was taken straight to the airplane in a little van, passing immigration at a special area used by visiting prime ministers, presidents, and high-level dignitaries. Liu and the woman boss with whom I had argued about torture weeks before followed me to the door of the airplane. We shook hands and I said my goodbye.

"Well, I can't say it was a fun experience, but at least it was a very interesting one."

Chapter 6
Collateral damage | **PAN JINLING**

Pan Jinling (潘锦玲), female, born 1987 in central China's Hubei province, moved to Beijing in 2014 to work with an app development company. Security agents abducted her at night from her home and placed her under Residential Surveillance at a Designated Location in January 2016 not for anything she had done but simply because she was the girlfriend of Swedish human rights activist Peter Dahlin (Chapter 5).

Pan is not a human rights activist. She is not a lawyer nor a journalist. She was not involved in Dahlin's work or with his NGO, China Action. Even so, she was disappeared, interrogated and held in solitary confinement for 23 days until the authorities had decided to deport her boyfriend.

On the day they finally came to take us, my boyfriend had already been extremely anxious for several days. I knew he had been working in human rights for a long time, and under a lot of pressure for a long time. He often referred to his anxiety as an "occupational disease." But on this day it was far worse than usual.

He had known for the past few days that his name was being mentioned to security agents at interrogations with rights lawyers he knew, and he had started destroying documents and papers. He had decided to leave China as soon as possible. Depending on how things developed, he wasn't sure if he'd ever be able to return.

It was a weekend, a Sunday I think, and I wanted to give him some space to deal with all the things he had to manage. I decided to go out for some fresh air.

Of course, I knew he worked on human rights issues, and that he had a lot of contact with lawyers around China. I also knew that this was not a very safe thing to be involved with in China, but I never thought any real danger would come from it; after all he was just helping Chinese lawyers use Chinese law. Still, he never told me very much about his work, never any details, so I didn't know much. Now, as I think back, I realize this secrecy was a way for him to protect me. In this way, in case anything happened, I would just be a nobody to the police. It was a good thing.

After leaving his house, I rode my bicycle to the third ring road and went to a movie. I found a huge supermarket, stocked with the kinds of imported things you can't find in a normal supermarket in Beijing. I wanted to get some things to make a nice dinner, using a favorite recipe from his mom.

After I left the market, I couldn't find my bicycle. I spent 10 minutes looking around outside the building where the other bicycles were but eventually gave up. I didn't want to waste any more time. As I got into a taxi, arms full of groceries for our dinner, without knowing why, I suddenly had a strange premonition. I shook it off and gave the driver our address.

Considering what would happen that evening, and knowing that I had been followed around for the previous few days, I now wonder if the police had anything to do with my missing bicycle. Had they taken it?

Once I got back, Peter told me he had changed his flight and was planning to leave that night. My thoughts swung between thinking he was overreacting and feeling a creeping sense of concern. My stomach tightened thinking about the strange premonition of my bicycle being stolen and the meaning it could portend.

The early evening was spent with him packing and finalizing data transfers and other computer issues, while I busied myself in the kitchen with his mom's recipe for creamy chicken pasta.

The air was heavy with concern and the later it got the more seriously I took the situation. I kept thinking, "What if he can never return, will we live together outside China?" In imagining the possibility of a life together in another country, I also wondered about my own work. What never entered my mind, not even as a flicker, was that I might also be detained or taken.

After dinner and when packing was finished, there were a few hours left before he had to leave for the airport, and maybe part with a city he had lived in for all these years, with all his friends, with no chance to say goodbye, or have a last stroll through the *hutongs* he loved so much. While we worried about his rushed departure, we still had no way of seeing what was coming.

We were snuggling together in bed, thinking about arrangements for our two cats, how I should quit my job, and what to do with his house. Where were we going to meet? And live? It felt like we had figured everything out, and I started to feel more relieved, the situation became less dark. Suddenly, everything changed.

You can often feel extra sensitive when you are nervous. I heard footsteps outside. Then, there was a loud knocking on the door, a thunderous clatter that shook us from the bed and made our hearts skip a beat. I couldn't help but think, "Is this it, the thing we have been dreading, is it actually happening right now?"

Peter opened the door. He seemed so calm. People squeezed through the door like water rushing with the rising tide. I jolted up in bed, wearing my sleeping clothes. My heart was racing but I had to tell myself to remain calm.

A dozen or more policemen streamed into the house. Someone had a video camera, and was recording the whole process. They must have really been planning this. I only later learned they were not regular police, but State Security.

We were told to change into normal clothing. I was surprised by how formal they were, presenting everything in accordance with the law. But how could this whole thing be in accordance with the law?

They read the detention notice, one for each of us. They presented warrants to search both of us, and the house. When they shouted out my name on the detention notice, it was so surreal to hear my full name called out by the police in this fashion, like they were talking about someone else. I wasn't myself; it was such a shock. I was being detained on suspicion of criminal activities endangering state security. I felt numb.

How did they know my name? Had they followed me, put me under surveillance? I had never noticed anything, and why would I? Why would I have thought I was being followed? Why would they follow me? My mind emptied itself of all thoughts and I was left standing in shock.

I knew Peter had planned ahead in case this ever happened to him. He had role played and practiced and studied accounts of other rights defenders so he could be better prepared in case the police came for him. Of course, we had never discussed it and I had no idea what to do, how to handle it, or what to expect. Peter remained calm, which at least gave me some comfort. I summoned all my strength. After all, I had done nothing wrong.

They wanted me to sign the warrants. Peter reminded me to make sure I fully understood any paperwork I was asked to sign before doing so. They were going to take me away now, they said. What was the point in signing the document? I was so confused. But I assumed being stubborn wouldn't help. I signed it after a few minutes. They confiscated my phone and a few other things and asked me again to sign a document confirming the confiscated items. I felt like I was being cut off from the world.

As they led me outside, they told me there was no need to take my bag or anything else. We are just going to ask a few questions, they said. A few female officers took me to a car in the small alley outside the house. They tried to blindfold me but I refused and they gave up.

Half an hour, one hour, an hour and a half, time dragged on as we sat in the car waiting, still parked, immobile. The officers were in the car with me. The women, in their 40s, looked like normal strangers you would see on the street. One of the two officers sitting on either side of me in the back fell asleep. What were we waiting for? Nobody said a word. Questions raced through my head at a pace only rivaled by my speeding heart.

A kind looking man from the neighborhood came up to the car and asked about my boyfriend's flight situation. Are they taking him to the airport? Strange, I thought.

Somehow, perhaps as the initial shock wore off, I fell asleep after maybe two hours of waiting in the stationary vehicle. When I woke up, the car was moving, and I realized we were part of a convoy of four or five cars moving together. I looked out of the tinted windows, through the dark Beijing night, searching the other cars, and was somewhat comforted thinking my boyfriend should be inside one of them.

It seemed like the cars were just driving in circles, maybe to make it harder for us to follow where they were taking us. Was it to one of the notorious Black Jails or a secret hotel? Was I just being used to trick my boyfriend or was my life going to end this way?

The place where I was taken was far outside of the city center, a building with four floors. We arrived. It felt like a scene from a mafia movie. As the gate opened, the camera team was already there, recording us as the car stopped. Then they changed and focused on another arriving car. I quietly sighed in relief, thinking that must be my boyfriend.

Four or five people took me to the third floor in an elevator. I was led into an interrogation room and put into a wooden chair. A board was locked over my legs. I couldn't move. There were heavy chains on the floor that I assumed were used to shackle people's ankles. Thankfully they didn't use them on me. The small red light on the camera in front of me indicated it was recording. There was a long table opposite me where the interrogator sat.

The interrogator told me they just wanted to ask me some questions and that I would be fine; hard to believe when I was strapped inside a chair that seemed more like a medieval torture device.

Since I had my own, regular job, and had nothing to do with my boyfriend's human rights work they must have just taken me to ask about him. I was shocked that they would take away my freedom, and treat me like a criminal, just to ask questions about my boyfriend. I stubbornly remained silent, thinking the less I spoke, the less chance I would have to make a mistake or risk my boyfriend's safety. I had no idea what to say or not say to help him but I figured silence wouldn't hurt.

I asked several times to call a colleague to explain that I would be absent from work the next day but my captors refused. I innocently pleaded that if I just disappeared my coworkers would start looking for me. They would go to the police. Wouldn't this cause trouble for you? I foolishly asked my interrogator. He made it clear that was not a problem; the police are their people. At that moment, I realized how naïve I had been about my own government, and how helpless I was in reality.

That night I didn't speak with them, but was made to sit, restrained, in the chair until 3 or 4 in the morning. They told me to rest, but that if I didn't speak it would just waste my time. After the first 24 hours, they said they could change my detention to Residential Surveillance at a Designated Location (RSDL) and keep me for six months! I was vaguely aware that 24 hours was a time limit for something, but that was about all I knew.

I was transferred to a room opposite the interrogation room. The entire room was padded. I assumed that was to make it impossible to commit suicide. I was too tired and fell asleep on the small bed in the corner. While sleeping, I half-dreamed I heard someone in high heels loudly stomping around in the corridor, my door opening and closing, and the high-heeled woman coming into my room to watch me.

The following evening they brought me back into the interrogation room. The first 24 hours had come and gone. They read an official declaration that I was being placed in RSDL. I was made to sign another paper. For a second, I wondered what would happen if I refused to sign.

Based on the name, Residential Surveillance, I thought at first it meant I was to be taken to my house, and just kept under house arrest. Little did I know that RSDL really means being put in a prison, the only difference being that an RSDL prison is secret and cut off from the world.

I was shown a paper about my rights and responsibilities. I asked about my right to hire a lawyer but was told that my case was an exception and that I was not allowed legal representation, nor was I to be allowed any form of communication with the outside world.

They did ask for my family's phone number, so they could notify them, but I would not be allowed to speak with them. My future looked very dark.

"I didn't do anything against the law," I found myself repeating constantly throughout my many interrogations. But each time they scoffed, "If you didn't do anything against the law, then why are you here?"

On the third day they brought me an orange-colored prison vest and told me to put it on. I felt a strong sense of shame—this is the kind of thing criminals wear. I am not a criminal. I assumed they wanted me to wear it as a way of breaking down my resistance, for my lack of cooperation.

I was very angry, and told them, "I will not wear it. I am not a criminal!" They tried a few more times, but eventually gave up after sending some messages on their phones.

Three or four days into my captivity, a woman, it seemed she was ranked higher that the others, came into my cell and told me I had no choice in the matter. I had to wear the orange vest and I had to wear it for another interrogation session that was going to start, she instructed matter-of-factly.

The interrogator was something of a "good cop." He didn't necessarily threaten me, just attempted simple mind games that didn't have much of an effect on me. He showed some receipts that my boyfriend had paid his ex-girlfriend, telling me that he was having an affair with her. He even showed me a photo of a baby he claimed they found in his wallet, saying he had a family outside China. I knew they were just trying to defame him, and didn't argue or disagree, choosing silence as my strategy. The whole thing just made it so clear to me what they were trying to achieve, but it had the opposite effect they were after. I would not betray him.

On the fourth day, the interrogation team changed. Another two plainclothes officers came in. They were far more imposing. Exuding power, the male interrogator lit a cigarette while his female counterpart stared me down with narrow, probing eyes. Their combined energy was tough. I realized they were probably going to be the "bad cops." I worried that they might torture me.

They worked well together, shouting at me, threatening me, and telling me how serious my situation was. They read the law I was supposed to have broken, a crime they said carries from five years to life imprisonment.

They told me my boyfriend had placed all responsibility on me—I knew this wasn't true. By warning me that I could be named as the mastermind they could threaten me with serious consequences if I didn't defend myself, that is, I should accuse my boyfriend to save myself. I remembered hearing somewhere that this is called the prisoner's dilemma.

The female officer made fun of me, attacking me for my disheveled appearance and trying other ways to shame me into cooperating. As I was restrained and surrounded, she could have probably said anything for this kind of verbal attack to have an emotional impact. But it didn't change the fact that I knew nothing. But they didn't want honesty, just a confession.

By the end of the interrogation session, my refusal to lie only enraged them. As the male interrogator left, he slammed the door with such force that I jolted in my restraints. They left me there, with a guard. It was very late by then.

I realized they were going to leave me there, strapped into the wooden chair all night. After some time, I was feeling exhausted but no sooner had I closed my eyes than the guard screamed into my face. I was shocked. The room had been quiet and for one second I had escaped behind closed eyes but the force of her violent outburst pulled me right back. Her face was even with mine. The room grew quiet again, and time passed in silence. Again, I felt myself nodding off, but as soon as my eyes were barely closed the guard was right there in my face screaming. This was how I passed the night, deprived of sleep. It was horrible.

That night, one sentence kept bouncing around in my head. They had told me, "You don't have to say what your boyfriend did, just say what you did." After being forced to keep my eyes open until morning, I told the guard to call in the interrogator. I would talk about myself, but they could not force me to say anything about my boyfriend. She agreed, and finally let me sleep.

After agreeing to speak about myself, I was handed back to the "good cop" team. A trick of course, and I knew it, but an effective tactic.

I was under watch 24 hours a day, every day. More than a dozen people would take turns, two at a time. They sat inside my cell and stared at me, taking notes on what I was doing, as if every small movement had to be recorded as evidence. So much attention.

I did some math; if each person was paid RMB6,000 a month [~USD1,000], and I was inside almost a month, the guards alone would have cost RMB60,000 at least [~USD10,000]. The cell was padded to prevent suicide, it had cameras, and the doors were always locked. What good were the guards? These guards, besides staring at me, also spent a lot of time with their phones just killing time, every day. There were several teams of interrogators, plus the facility itself, food, and everything else. I wasn't even seriously thought of as a criminal, just bait really to lure my boyfriend into a trap, but all the money the government wasted on keeping me for a month, the people's money. For what? To show power and strength? But how powerful could they really be if I was seen as a threat? It made me smile a little inside.

Many of the guards seemed to be just students, or very young recruits, like simple country bumpkins.

There was an older woman who liked to chat and often spoke with the others when it was their turn to watch me. I realized this was just a job for her. She wasn't a police officer but an ordinary citizen paid to monitor secret detainees with the same level of devotion as if she was a bank teller or a janitor. She spoke with a low voice, but in the small room I could hear her well. She spoke with the other guards about investments, about buying a house, other gossip. In my boredom I eavesdropped, but I guess they didn't care.

There was another one; she was always aggressive. She would tell me she would throw away my food if I didn't eat it quickly enough.

A young girl, who also looked like she had been plunked down in this place from the countryside, always shouted at me if I stayed too long in bed. She refused to allow me to take showers. She was so bitter.

Another older, scowling woman yelled at me and kept me from opening the curtains when I tried to let in some sunlight. Most of the time they kept the heavy curtains closed, the room illuminated by uncomfortable fluorescent lights day and night. The whole night.

Not all of my guards were mean. The older lady who liked to gossip sometimes asked what I wanted to eat, if I wanted a bigger portion, or some extra fruit. Sometimes, she would even bring me water without me having to ask for it. Despite the food remaining similar day in day out, I would finish everything, and came to enjoy the eating time very much, except when dinner was only soggy, soupy noodles.

After a week and a half or so, when it seemed they believed they couldn't get any information from me—I really didn't have anything to tell them anyway—the attitude of the guards seemed to change. Even the mean woman who had thrown the vest at me started behaving more nicely. She asked about my yoga practice, some of which I would do by my bed to pass time. After their change of tone, I was free to open the curtains and see sunlight as I pleased.

Another thing that changed was that now when they thought I was just the girlfriend of a human rights worker, not a human rights worker myself, they wanted to change my way of thinking, to convince me I was wasting my time with him.

They spent a lot of time defaming my boyfriend, telling me how important it is to be proud of being Chinese, to love the government, and not get involved in sensitive issues. They wasted even more time and money calling the local police in my hometown, who actually travelled all the way to Beijing to try and convince me that I was in the wrong, that my boyfriend was an anti-China force, and a spy. They had evidence of all of this, they claimed. His purpose was to destroy China and start a color revolution. I was Chinese; I could not support an outsider. I had to wonder how much of this they honestly believed or if they were just playing their parts.

This role especially fell to the female "good cop." She would often come to have personal chats with me in my room, trying to convince me that it wasn't worth protecting my boyfriend because he is an outsider. She tried to show real concern, as if she said these things because she wanted the best for me. All very convincing, but a trick nonetheless.

When it seemed like they had decided I wasn't a criminal, and that I should be set free at some point, I let them play their games and pretended I was considering everything they said.

During the final two weeks, the male "good cop" became my main conversation partner. Towards the end of my 23 days, he told me my boyfriend was going to be deported, and that after that I would also be set free. Throughout the whole time, they continued to defame him. I didn't care, and I didn't argue. The only thing that meant anything to me was that both of us were going to get out of there. They could go on about him being a spy however much they wanted, as long as we were getting out.

After I knew I would be set free and my boyfriend would be deported, I started having real trouble sleeping. Knowing the ordeal would come to an end made time move so much more slowly.

I often just stood at the window looking out at a field filled with abandoned buses nearby. There was a bird's nest in one of the few trees close by in the walled-in yard below. The sun would set around 5:45pm every day. The slower time moved, the more I noticed little things.

Sometimes the 25 minutes it took for the sun to set felt like 25 years. I found inspiration in the trees and the sunset and made a drawing. I asked the "good cop" to give it to my boyfriend, which he did. I was surprised actually. In the final days, I looked forward to the "good cop" coming by my room, as I thought any day now he would come and say that it was finally over. In the end, he was the one to bring the news of our release.

I was told I was being taken to my boyfriend's house to collect some items for him to take with him, that he was going to be deported from China. It was the first time I was let outside in almost a month. They said it was the coldest day of winter that day and although I was surrounded by guards and blindfolded, the crisp air felt beautiful as I inhaled a gulp of freedom before being shoved into the car and taken to his house.

Inside, Peter's house was just as cold as the outside. It was freezing. The house was filled with unwashed dishes and things scattered around, left in the haste of the raid. It felt desolate, knowing he would never see his home again, and we would never be together here again. I was told I could pack a bag of things for him and that they would give it to him.

I asked to meet him before he was deported. After going through this most important event of our lives, we needed to confirm our feelings for each other. I needed to see him, to know how he was.

They blindfolded me again and took me to a meeting room. When I arrived he was there, waiting. His beard had grown so long he looked like a wild jungle hunter and had clearly lost some weight. We hugged each other more tightly than I think we had ever done before, tighter than I thought was possible. I was happy with tears. We sat down with a few officers monitoring us; as usual there was never any privacy. It felt good that we confirmed that we were still alive and that our plans were the same.

The last day came, and I was given a paper to sign in which I had to agree not to give any interviews and some other rules to follow after I was released. They asked me where I wanted to be dropped off. I would have to wait until my boyfriend had been deported before being taken down to a car in the garage, blindfolded, and driven back into central Beijing.

Once we got into the city, I was allowed to take off my blindfold. It was first time I saw tall buildings after so many days confined in a small room. It felt fresh and heavy. I had a smile on my face. It felt that everyone in the car was relaxed, they even chatted amongst themselves about everyday things. The "good cop" asked me about my plans, and before arriving at the drop off point, gave me his phone number, and asked me to report back when I had decided what I was going to do.

After I got out, I watched the car drive away, only to get quickly stuck in traffic. For a few moments, I watched the vehicle in traffic, realizing that if I hadn't gone through this experience I would never have looked at a car like that and imagined the kind of power the people inside possess. The car and its inhabitants looked so normal, and yet they were not.

There was nothing normal about any of this.

Chapter 7
Your only right is to obey | **XIE YANG**

Xie Yang (谢阳), male, born 1972, is a prominent rights defense lawyer based in central Hunan province. He has worked extensively in rights defense, including representing members of the civil rights group New Citizens' Movement and the China Democracy Party, as well as persecuted Christians and victims of illegal land grabs.

In 2015, the authorities targeted Xie in the "709 Crackdown" against lawyers and activists, placing him under Residential Surveillance at a Designated Location. Like many victims of RSDL, the police hounded Xie's family so that his wife, Chen Guiqiu, eventually fled China with their two children in early 2017. They now live in exile in the US. After a secret trial in May 2017, Xie was released from detention but was not freed; he was placed under heavy police surveillance at his home in Hunan.

Xie Yang's story is based on the vivid testimony of torture in RSDL he told his lawyers, and interviews conducted by Safeguard Defenders with family members and lawyers.

"You are now under Residential Surveillance in a Designated Location. Your only right is to obey."

Two days earlier, Xie had traveled to Hongjiang to represent a group of farmers over a land dispute. "There was nothing different about this time. He simply left for work like before," his wife Chen Guiqiu recalled. "There was no reason to think that things were dangerous or different than other times, or that this would happen."

In the early hours, asleep in his hotel room, a group of men, some in uniform and others in plainclothes, forced their way inside. They confiscated everything, his phone, laptop, lawyer's license, wallet; it was all taken as evidence. They took him to the local police station with his assistant, Wei Deifeng, who was released after 24 hours.

They arrived at the station at around 6 in the morning. They promptly shackled Xie to a chair and abandoned him to his thoughts. Several hours later, two officers with out-of-town accents, came into the room to begin the interrogation. They asked about his involvement in the Human Rights Lawyers Group, an unofficial network of lawyers in China established to exchange information and provide case support (separate from the Hong Kong-based NGO, China Human Rights Lawyers Concern Group). Xie, at first, denied any knowledge of the group. Even just the existence of unofficial associations is seen as a threat to the dominance of the Party.

"The lawyers in that group are anti-Party and anti-socialist in nature." The interrogators pressed him, demanding that Xie withdraw from the network and its WeChat group. They added that if Xie cooperated with them and quit the Human Rights Lawyers Group, he would be treated leniently. They said the authorities were in the process of rounding up lawyers across the country and that he was risking punishment if he didn't cooperate. Xie agreed to make a brief statement, expecting they would keep their promise and treat him leniently.

Minutes later, a senior official came into the room, saying he was dissatisfied with Xie's attitude. He wanted a new statement and demanded access to his mobile device. Xie refused.

Xie spent the night shackled in the police station, denied sleep. If he tried to close his eyes, an officer would slap and shake him awake. The following morning, he was shown a copy of the decision to place him under Residential Surveillance at a Designated Location and then taken away.

Xie was moved from the police station to a hotel, or more accurately, a government-run guesthouse, the type scattered across the country and often used to hold people outside of normal judicial process, in other words a Black Jail. Escorted roughly by several officers, he was forced into the room that would be his home for the next six months. There was a camera on the wall. His only roommates would be the three "chaperones," as he called them, and the many agents tasked with his endless surveillance and grueling interrogations.

For hours, Xie was subjected to a rotating barrage of questions; groups of officers kept coming, two at a time, sometimes three or more. They asked the same questions, took no notes; it was more an onslaught to wear him down than to glean information. Xie said he later discovered that more than 40 people interrogated him.

That evening, a high-level official from the Changsha Domestic Security Unit came to welcome him. He hadn't slept for over 30 hours. They knew it.

"If we think two hours of sleep a day is enough, then you get two hours of sleep. If we think one hour is enough, you get one hour. If we think half an hour is enough, you get half an hour. If we think five minutes is enough, then you get five minutes."

"You are now under Residential Surveillance in a Designated Location. Your only right is to obey."

For days, Xie was forced to sit on a "dangling chair," a crude torture device composed of plastic stools piled up on each other, where he was sometimes kept for up to 20 hours a day. The stools have no backs and are stacked high to prevent the legs from reaching the ground. Hanging in this way slowly constrains the blood flow, and causes escalating pain and swelling in the legs and back. The swelling begins at the feet and slowly creeps upwards until the body is engulfed in pain. Xie pleaded with them; he told them that he had a preexisting leg injury. This kind of torture, he explained in vain, would cripple him. They reacted with callous indifference, responding, "Don't give us conditions. You'll do what we tell you to do!"

When he failed to answer their questions the way they wanted, his interrogators would fly into a rage. They would drag his body from the stools, and fling him into a corner of the room outside the surveillance cameras' field of vision. With one officer holding his arms, another would kick, punch and knee him. But they were always careful to avoid leaving visible marks; they spared his face and concentrated on delivering their blows to his body. At other times, Xie was hung from the ceiling and beaten. He lost consciousness at one point.

When he was confined to the dangling chair, the guards made sure he couldn't move or shift position to stimulate even a trickle of blood flow or to stretch out a cramped and swollen muscle. Any time Xie attempted to adjust his legs or lower his head, a guard standing behind him beat him on the back of his head, and shouted, "If you move at all, we can consider you to be attacking us and we can use whatever means we need to subdue you. We're not gentle with people who attack police officers!"

The physical pain was combined with humiliation. Xie was forced to request permission to use the toilet or have a drink of water. He was made to go for long periods without any water. They would place a bottle or a cup in front of him but would not let him drink. This control over his basic needs, he remembered, made him miserable. Once he grabbed a bottle and started drinking only to have it forcefully snatched from his hands. He was beaten while the guard accused him of having tried to attack a police officer.

He would sit suffering on the dangling chair, while three or four interrogators surrounded him. One would stand directly in the front, demanding answers. There was always one staring at him from the side and another lurking behind, primed to beat him and bark out orders to "Sit up straight," or some other command.

Other times, a few of his captors would sit by his side, each with several lit cigarettes held together and puff great clouds of asphyxiating smoke into his face. When he protested, they responded, "What can you do about it? We'll smoke like this if we want to!" This wasn't done to elicit a confession, Xie explained. "Just to torment me and make me miserable."

They called this the "furnace" and after his first week, if the interrogators thought he wasn't cooperating they would threaten to send him back to the furnace. The threat of torture was always there. They made sure he knew it.

"Xie Yang, we'll torture you to death just like an ant," they threatened.

Adept in stoking despair, several interrogators would often call Xie's attention to the silence of the facility, the isolation and lack of noise from the outside, noting that the walls had been constructed to shield all sound from traveling out. The threat was clear: it was hopeless to wish for salvation. They continued.

"Don't think you'll get out of here and be able to file a complaint." They explained, "This case comes from Beijing. We're handling your case on behalf of Party Central. Even if we were to kill you, they wouldn't find a single piece of evidence to prove it was us who did it."

Xie later recalled in tears, thinking about his disappearance, "If they tortured me to death, my family wouldn't even know."

It wasn't until four days after he had been taken from the hotel in Hongjing, that Xie's wife received notice of her husband's fate. A letter, arriving at their home, alerted her that Xie was being held under RSDL. Reading the notice, she explained, "I didn't even know what RSDL was."

It would be several days before the pieces started falling into place, as she learned that since 9 July many others had been taken from around the country. This was the start of the "709 Crackdown." It was about a lot more than just Xie Yang. But this only made her feel worse, more concerned, and shocked at the scope of the campaign.

"The more I learned about this being part of something bigger, the more worried I became," she explained. Her worries increased and began to be mixed with anger after a lawyer she met in a restaurant explained more about RSDL. How else could she feel? She was denied any contact with her husband; his lawyers were prevented from meeting with him; the state tightly concealed Xie's fate and whereabouts.

Xie's early days in RSDL passed in relatively uniform torment, with five regular shift changes throughout a 24-hour period. For the first four shifts, from 8am until 3am, he was generally confined to the dangling chair and subjected to endless interrogations. They informed him he could sleep from 3am until 6:30am but this was never the case as his interrogators would drag the session on until after 4am. For many nights in a row he was only allowed to sleep around two hours a night.

The use of the dangling chair and sleep deprivation serves a clear purpose for the state torturer. It is a slow form of torture that builds to excruciating levels but leaves no physical marks. It assaults the body and spirit with patient precision, while leaving no evidence behind.

There is no way to describe it, said Xie. After three days of such treatment, he had a complete mental breakdown. When his tormentors arrived, because he was already in such a disturbed mental state, he began to cry. He begged them to let him sleep but they refused, demanding that instead of respite he must write a statement. He could barely lift a pen, he pleaded. After they had removed him from the dangling chair so he could write the statement, Xie tried to put his head on the table to rest, but they seized his collar and jerked him up.

"If you're not going to write, then tonight you don't get to sleep!" They yelled at him. Barely capable of writing a statement, much less comprehending what he wrote due to his exhaustion, Xie was punished by being forced to stay awake the whole night. At dawn, the interrogation resumed.

"Each day's interrogation was full of these kinds of threats, insults, and reprimands. It was too much!" Xie recalled.

"I sleep very well during the day," an interrogator mocked him at the start of one evening session. "Then I get so excited every night at this time because I get to torment you. You see, I'm going to torment you until you go insane. Don't even imagine that you'll be able to walk out of here and continue being a lawyer. You're going to be a cripple."

They wanted Xie to admit to all the crimes they put before him, but even more, they wanted to break him until he didn't just agree to the charges but believed them.

He was given three choices for his confession, three options to explain what they claimed were his crimes: that he did it for fame, he did it for profit, or he did it to oppose the Party and socialism.

"This is a case of counterrevolution! Do you think the Communist Party will let you go? I could torture you to death and no one could help you."

His worst "crime," the counterrevolution, and the focus of many nights of repeated interrogations and torture, was his involvement in the informal network of Chinese lawyers, the China Human Rights Lawyers Group. For any reasonable person, this was just a group of individual lawyers embracing the freedom of association to work together, to protect each other, and to provide mutual support for each other's work. For the Communist Party, however, they are an organized opposition force, an imaginary threat to their continued grip on power because in their mind independent lawyers threaten their attempts to rule through the use of the law.

"It made me angrier and angrier when I started to learn about RSDL," Chen explained, and as she learned more she realized how futile it was for her to expect the law to help Xie's situation. Reading and researching more about RSDL online, and hearing the stories of others placed in RSDL, made her feel increasingly powerless. "There is no way to deal with it according to the law. No mechanisms, no supervision, no appeal, nothing. They just took him and there is nothing anyone can do at all."

On the outside, Chen was frantically searching for a way to help her husband. Inside RSDL, his captors did not confine their torture to physical and mental abuse targeting Xie alone.

Xie's tormentors threatened to expand their barbarous reach to his family. They made it clear they could ruin the lives of anyone close to him.

"Your wife is a professor at Hunan University—surely she must have 'economic problems'? If you don't cooperate, we might be forced to expand this matter. If you don't come clean and explain things clearly, we'll go after your wife without a doubt."

"And we know your brother is a civil servant, a minor official. Surely he has some problems we could investigate? And we know you have a nephew who has bright prospects and works at the Hunan Bureau of Letters and Visits [an office that deals with petitioners' complaints]. Is he really uncorrupt? Don't force us to go and investigate him."

"Your daughter is a student at Bocai Middle School in Changsha. If her classmates and teachers knew that her father was a counterrevolutionary, could she even raise her head up? How could she ever get a job as a civil servant in the future?"

They issued direct threats. "Your wife and children need to pay attention to traffic safety when they're out in the car. There are a lot of traffic accidents these days."

"It would be easy for us to expand the scope of our investigation. We have plenty of resources. If you don't cooperate with us, we can investigate your friends, one by one, and put them through the wringer. We've got the resources and we have our methods. In this case, there's no limit to how far we can take the investigation—and that includes your law firm, your friends and your colleagues. We'll go after whomever we please and deal with them however we want."

After several months inside his secret prison, one day in late October, Xie began to shiver uncontrollably and he broke out in a cold sweat. Gripped by fear for his life, Xie asked his captors to take him to a hospital. But such contact with the outside world would defeat the brutal efficiency of an enforced disappearance and the officials refused his request. Instead, they promised to have someone come and examine him. Xie did not trust any doctor they sent.

Xie was afraid again that he was going to die, and that his wife and daughters wouldn't know. He sobbed as he recalled these details.

Seeing some people outside the window, Xie shouted out his wife's name and work unit, her telephone number and begged them to contact her. "This is Lawyer Xie Yang! I'm being held here by the Changsha Domestic Security Police! No one has notified my family! Please let my wife know that I'm ill and need medical treatment!"

That evening, waiting for an ambulance that eventually came and left without providing him any relief, a burly man in civilian clothes came in and walked right up to Xie. He abruptly shoved him against the wall with a hefty blow, knocking the wind out of him. Pinning him with one paw, he slapped him several times across the face. Xie was left in a semi-conscious state, his breath short in his compressed chest from the force of the man's throttling.

After six months in RSDL, Xie Yang was formally arrested in January 2016 on suspicion of "inciting subversion," and transferred out of RSDL. Even so, for months he was denied any contact with the outside world. In July 2016, Xie was finally allowed to meet his then lawyers, Lin Qilei and Zhang Chongshi, who would later be illegally dismissed by the authorities. But this first meeting was just a ploy by the state, hoping to manipulate the lawyers into convincing their client to confess. Instead the lawyers listened as Xie told them how he had been tortured under RSDL and again after being transferred into a formal criminal detention center.

Around the time of one of these meetings, on 21 November, human rights lawyer Jiang Tianyong also disappeared. Jiang had been helping Xie Yang's wife and disseminating information about his torture.

Stories of Xie's torture spread quickly on Chinese social media and his situation slowly began to receive mounting international attention. When another lawyer, Chen Jiangang, first got wind of the news, he explained he didn't pay much attention. He reposted it on social media but avoided thinking about it much more because he felt helpless. "I had learned long ago that there was no evil deed, and no act too immoral, for this dictatorship."

After the authorities had forced Xie's first lawyers to abandon his case, his wife contacted Chen Jiangang asking him to take over her husband's legal defense. Chen recalled her reminding him that he would likely face enormous pressure, potentially violent reprisal, and cautioned him to think over his decision carefully before agreeing.

Chen, along with another lawyer, Liu Zhengqing, met with Xie Yang for the first time on 23 December 2016. They met him again a few more times in January during which time Xie provided a detailed account of how he had suffered, which is the basis of this chapter. The exchange was meticulously transcribed and signed by Xie.

At one of these meetings, Xie also gave Chen a handwritten note explaining that if he ever confessed or admitted to any crimes in court it would have been because he was coerced.

The full transcript of their conversation was published at the China Change website on 19 January 2017. The shocking details of Xie's treatment attracted international attention and condemnation.

In March 2017, China responded to growing diplomatic pressure by launching a smear campaign and media war against the lawyers who had exposed Xie's torture. For several weeks, Chinese state media published articles and televised broadcasts in English and Chinese calling the torture allegations, "nothing but cleverly orchestrated lies."

As a principle target of the state's campaign, Chen Jiangang shot back with an article of his own refuting the state's empty denials of torture and ill-treatment. China's propaganda campaign also targeted Jiang Tianyong, who had been disappeared months earlier and had no way of countering the state's propaganda.

After enduring more than a year of fear and harassment, Xie's wife Chen said she had lost hope. It was time to think of their children. In March 2017 she decided it was no longer safe for her or her children to remain in China. A week later, they set off on their escape to the United States. One of their daughters holds US citizenship. With little time to plan, they made their way to Thailand by land with flight tickets booked to travel from Bangkok to the United States.

One more disaster befell them. When they were trapped in a Thai immigration detention center, some 10 Chinese agents encircled the facility. The fear that they would be repatriated to China swelled inside her; if things had been bad before, forced repatriation would guarantee their treatment would be far worse. In the end, at the eleventh hour, US diplomats intervened and secured the family's release, escorting them to the airport in Bangkok. But a faceoff between Thai, US, and Chinese officials ensued, which nearly escalated into a physical confrontation. In the end, Chen and her daughters made it onto their flight and escaped the long arm of China.

They are lucky, but the wives and children of many other courageous rights defenders who have been disappeared or sentenced to lengthy prison sentences have not been so fortunate. In this, we are reminded that enforced disappearances and reprisals do not target only one individual but entire families and communities.

Chapter 8
If you want to come back alive | JIANG XIAOYU

Jiang Xiaoyu (江孝宇), male, born 1980, lives in Beijing where he works in IT and systems administration. He got involved with rights work in the early 2000s when he himself was a petitioner. Because he could speak fluent English, he started helping Chinese human rights defenders communicate with foreign journalists and diplomats.

Security agents seized Jiang in 2016 and starved and beat him for a weekend in an underground prison in the outskirts of Beijing. Jiang was not formally placed under Residential Surveillance at a Designated Location (RSDL), but he was repeatedly threatened that he could be disappeared under RSDL if he didn't cooperate.

Jiang Xiaoyu is a pseudonym. Some of the details in his story have been changed to protect his identity out of concern for his safety. However, the account of his treatment in state custody has been left unaltered.

It had been about a week since the disappearance of a close friend of mine. In those days, rights defenders were disappearing left and right but this time it was someone I had known for years. I knew that I too would be taken. I had already burned some sensitive papers about the work we had done together. On several successive afternoons and early evenings, I had torn pages into strips and shoved them into a small bin, the kind kept around for burning spirit money at Qingming [also called Tomb Sweeping Day, when people honor their ancestors by sprucing up their grave sites]. I had disposed of several wads of paperwork like this but there was too much to carry on in this fashion. One midnight, I dumped the rest in the compression pit of the garbage disposal station. Rushing around like that made me nervous, very nervous.

I considered flying out of China immediately to escape, but I thought about all the rights defenders [such as Ilham Tohti and Cao Shunli] I had heard of that had been detained or disappeared from the airport. It wasn't really an option and I gave up on the idea.

I had already talked with a rights lawyer about power of attorney. I contacted an old friend from the rights movement, someone I trusted a great deal and who had already been out of China for a few years. I explained my concerns, what I wanted for myself and for my family. If I lost my freedom, I explained, I wanted to avoid any international attention, assuming this might help to protect my family. I asked for assistance in getting them out of the country.

I had given up trying to save myself, having made arrangements as best as I could for my family, and resigned myself to wait for the police to come.

On the Saturday I was taken I had been home all day. My wife and our young daughter were spending the day in the countryside outside Beijing. The last thing I wanted was for my daughter to see the police come for her daddy.

I had spent the week increasingly debilitated by anxiety and insomnia, unable to eat properly, so that by that Saturday I was completely drained. I tried to nap but it was impossible to fall asleep. I couldn't shake the suspicion that someone was outside. Every time I tried to get comfortable on the bed, I was sure they would come. My anxiety was intolerable. How many times did I get up, pace the room, look out the window, only to sit down and then start the whole process again? When they finally came, it was terrifying, but in a way at least, it was a release from the mental torment of waiting.

They came in the afternoon. I didn't hear anything outside but as soon as my dog started barking like crazy, a part of me knew. I left the bedroom and walked tentatively toward the front door. I could clearly see seven or eight figures huddled on the other side. I opened the door and unable to hold back my nervous reflex, I blurted out, "Here you are!" They presented their ID cards, not police but State Security. I wanted to appear cooperative, "Please come in but do not alarm my neighbors. I don't want this to affect my family."

There was only one uniformed policeman but he left quickly after the group had entered my house. He must have been a local police officer sent to assist in my capture. Perhaps, after seeing me so cooperative, they didn't need him anymore and they let him go. The rest were in plainclothes, one of them filmed me the whole time with a video camera. Another one took photographs.

They treated me respectfully while they were inside my house. There was no violence or raised voices, maybe because I was cooperating. The first thing they did after entering was to demand my cellphone. They announced that I was being detained on suspicion of supporting crimes that endangered national security. They made me sign a detention notice, and proceeded to conduct an extensive search of my house.

They were meticulous, writing down and taking photos of anything they thought might be useful. They found some old phones and old batteries that I had forgotten about. While they searched they asked me random questions, such as what time had I woken up that day, what had I been doing before they arrived. Thinking back on it now,

I realize they probably already knew what I had in my possession, likely even knew what I had been doing all morning, and the week before. They must have been watching me. I comforted myself by thinking that they intentionally chose the moment when my daughter was away with her mother. I was thankful for that, at least.

They had been at it for almost three hours, searching my house. It was starting to get dark. I panicked. I was worried that my daughter might return. If she came home to this she would be shocked. I asked if I could call my wife. The leader of the group, a man with glasses, who I would see many more times over the coming few days, considered my request and then handed me my phone. "Don't try any funny business," he warned. I called my wife, asking where she was. "No rush to get back. Stay a bit longer," I told her and ended the call. I think she understood.

Despite having bought more time, my mind was blank while they rummaged through my house. I wasn't afraid for myself, but worried about my daughter. When she returns, how will she feel seeing all this mess? It felt like a horrible dream.

As the search continued, they would ask me to identify several items that they thought were suspect. I answered, only half aware of what I was being asked or what I was saying. One thing that surprised me was the box of business cards they found, cards I had collected mostly in meetings with diplomats and people in the human rights field. It was clear I hadn't thought about them in a long time, as the box had gathered that layer of dust all too common on things out of use in Beijing. I had completely forgotten about them, but State Security reacted as though they had found valuable evidence against me.

Not long after discovering the business cards, the investigators seemed content with what they had found so far. They had written a long list of confiscated items. They had even confiscated my six-year-old daughter's iPad. How absurd. It was just a toy for a child. I tried to explain this to them, hoping they would leave it. But the man with glasses was unmoved. They put the iPad into a bag with the business cards and other items they had taken.

Once they had completed the house search, they told me they were taking me away. I requested that they not handcuff me while I was still in my house so that my neighbors wouldn't be alarmed. I was hoping to protect my family. They agreed, saying that they didn't want a scene either. They took me out and down the stairs.

That was the last time that I still half believed I was going to be okay.

When we arrived downstairs, they spread out, with one officer walking in front, and one behind me. We reached a black Audi—it didn't even have government license plates. They put me in the middle of the back seat, with an officer on either side of me. My wrists were bound in handcuffs but they let me rest my hands comfortably on my lap until we had exited the complex.

As soon as we had passed through the gates, the guards removed my glasses and slipped a thick black hood over my head. Everything was obscured. They made me raise my arms and place my handcuffed hands behind my head. It was extremely uncomfortable, and in the total darkness frightening, but I was forced to maintain this position until we arrived at the detention center.

My head was covered but I could sense that the car was slowing down at a tollgate. No one spoke and we sped away. A voice addressed me, my head still covered but I identified the voice as the man with glasses. "Jiang, we are crossing the mountains. If you want to come back alive, you should think well about what you tell us." I answered that I understood.

He mentioned someone I knew who had disappeared a few days earlier, trying to get me to denounce him, saying he was engaged in activities that endangered national security. I refused. He pressed on, but was frustrated by my refusal. I could hear a body shifting in the seat in front of me, and then a sudden spike of pain across my hooded face. He had punched me. The rest of the ride was spent in silence; a few tears rolled down my face.

With the hood covering my head, I couldn't see anything, but I could feel the change in light that seemed to indicate we were entering a basement car park. I was taken out of the car, hood still on, and led to what I assumed must be an interrogation room.

After we arrived, they didn't allow me to remove the hood so I still couldn't see anything, but I could listen to what was happening around me. They were processing the handover. I was made to sit for a long time before they finally removed the hood.

After so long in darkness, the bright lights were painful to my eyes. It was startling and uncomfortable. As my eyes adjusted to the sudden brightness, I began to look around. I saw that I was sitting in a wooden interrogation chair. There was a table across from me. There were several cameras pointing at me, one in the middle of the interrogation table, two on the ceiling, and one behind me. The walls were padded.

They didn't interrogate me immediately, but made me sit and wait.

There was an older guard whose job was to monitor me. He didn't talk to me; he was just sat there reading a book by himself. I didn't see the name of the book clearly because they had not returned my glasses. In fact, I couldn't see much of anything because of my poor eyesight. At one point, I protested that I couldn't see anything but it didn't matter to them. In fact, they seemed to delight in my uneasiness. They didn't return my glasses throughout the entire time they detained me, not even when they forced me to sign my name on the interrogation notes. I was forced to look very closely, my nose on the paper, to make sure that I understood, before signing.

After a couple of hours, two people came into the room. One of them was the same man with the glasses from before. The interrogation lasted until midnight. They dug into every detail of my life, asking about everything I had done since I was born. They asked what I had studied in school, where my relatives worked, what kinds of people I knew, and how I got to know them. The man with the glasses, who must have been the leader, was very nasty.

"Your studies were quite good during your childhood. How did you step onto the road of crime?" I protested that I was not guilty; that nothing I had done was illegal.

He shot back, "If that's so, then how come you are here with me interrogating you?"

Sometimes he made a ferocious face, trying to intimidate me. Especially when he tried to force me to admit that people I respected were secretly working with foreign forces to destabilize China, but I firmly refused.

He shouted hysterically, "Do you want your daughter to be kicked out of kindergarten? I'm telling you, even if you want to be some kind of hero and stay in prison, your wife and daughter would live miserable lives. I can make it so that no school will accept your daughter ever! If you think they can escape, I can make it so that they never leave the country!"

The other person in the interrogation room didn't talk much. He stood there taking notes while the man with glasses berated me and threatened my family. A few times he spoke up, softly, as if to make me think he was on my side, trying to persuade me that if I wanted to get out all I needed to do was to cooperate. The sooner I cooperated, the sooner I would be released.

There were no real changes throughout the first night of my interrogation. They seemed to be asking me the same questions over and over again, always circling back to get me to admit that this one devoted human rights defender I know is really just a spy.

At some point in the evening, they changed interrogators. The new team was somewhat comic, one fat and one skinny. The fat man was definitely the "bad cop."

The fat man launched into questions about the business cards they had found in my house. He picked up each card, took a moment to examine it, and then showed it to me, demanding to know how I met such and such a person. I could barely see because I wasn't allowed to wear my glasses so he kept almost shoving the cards into my face so I could try and make out the names. Most of them were the cards of diplomats, lawyers, or NGO workers I had met over the years. Most of them I honestly couldn't remember where or how I had met. I couldn't answer his questions. I truthfully had no memory of every single person, but my failure to give answers only enraged him as he assumed I was lying.

The fat man shouted, "Don't try to think that you will be fine without telling us. We can destroy you over these cards!"

To me, this didn't make any sense. How could a box full of

business cards prove anything?

He continued, "What kind of person would have contact with these people? Don't you know how these diplomats and NGOs operate? They are all spies!"

I tried to explain that I really wasn't familiar with them, that they are just cards I had received when meeting these people for the first time and that I had never contacted any of them afterwards. I explained that sometimes rights defenders or civil society groups asked me to help interpret at meetings with foreigners but I didn't keep in regular contact. And anyway, I thought, so what if I met some diplomats once in a while. Was that a crime?

He was especially interested in the cards belonging to a US Embassy official. I explained that I didn't have any contact with the Embassy. I didn't even remember the person whose card it was. I must have gotten it at some meeting, I told him, several years before. That was the truth. But, of course, he didn't believe me and remained angry, his nostrils flared.

I was exhausted. The interrogation had been going on for some 12 hours, non-stop. I couldn't talk any longer. My exhaustion must have shown. The fat man said mockingly, "I can see you are tired. Let's go wash your face and wake you up."

I was taken into a bathroom opposite the interrogation room. Naively, I had just splashed a handful of water on my face thinking nothing of it when the fat man cornered me. He punched me hard. I was in shock.

He started beating me, shouting, "Still can't think clearly? You will never escape!"

At first, I tried protecting myself from his fists but it was futile. He beat me mercilessly. I was crumpled on the floor at the side of the toilet, crying and pleading, "I don't know. I don't know. It won't work even if you beat me to death."

At this point, the other one came and pulled the fat man off me. The thinner man took me out of the bathroom. I don't know how long the beating had lasted. I was stunned. Later, I thought about how skilled the fat man was at beating people without leaving any marks. I didn't have any bruises. My torso burned but there were no visible bruises to match how I felt. It was painful and humiliating. I was alone and powerless.

The fat man embraced his evil role. He beat me several more times while interrogating me. It was always the same, lengthy and exhausting, repetitive questioning until I could barely focus. My head would ache, my eyes droop, and then he would beat me. Each time it sent me into a spiral of shock and shame. It is hard to describe.

Finally, around 7 or 8 the following morning, the fat man and his partner left. I was relieved because I hoped that meant the end of my beatings. My whole body hurt. For a while it was just me and the older man with his book. He sat silently reading and watching me. It was hell and I hoped they would let me sleep, but instead of rest the man with the glasses came back.

I had been awake all night, questioned and beaten many times. I was tired and needed food. I asked the man with the glasses if I could have breakfast. With a nasty smile he shot back, "You don't get food if you don't cooperate. We are not going to feed you now. And if you continue to be uncooperative, we won't even give you water."

Despite that first assault in the car on the way to the detention facility, the man with the glasses never really beat me again. I was thankful he was not like his fat counterpart. But for sure I suffered in other ways during his interrogations.

I think with all the shock, physical and emotional, I was even more starving. Later, after another session of the same questions, I asked the man with the glasses to please let me eat lunch. His face contorted in the same wicked smugness as he spoke, "We went on too late today. The food is already finished. You can hold onto your hunger."

Later, he switched tactics. He stopped his circular questioning and started saying that I had been sold out. At this point I realized several other people I had worked with must have been taken. Knowing all these different partners were in police custody at the same time made my head spin—how was I supposed to navigate my interrogation without knowing what other people had said or not said.

He wanted me to think the others had pinned all the blame on me, to save themselves, and that my only chance of escape was to denounce them. He said, "We know the others don't really speak English. So, all communication with foreigners you people have must pass through you. You pass messages from outsiders to your partners but they don't know how you communicate with these foreigners. That's why you have these business cards. Admit it."

He wanted me to admit that I was a major decision maker, and that in the end I was responsible for everything. I was in serious trouble but if I denounced the others, the man with the glasses promised that things would be easy for me. It was a trick, a lie.

I had no problem admitting that I did some translation work, sometimes interpreted during a meeting with a diplomat, which is why I had the business cards. But I had no real idea about any other projects: who had designed them or where the money came from. How could I know about all the cases human rights lawyers worked on? I was just a simple translator. How could I be a major player in China's human rights movement?

I had a full-time job, working in IT for a successful company, which meant I worked all the time, every damn day. Where would I have found the time to mastermind anything, or to be involved anymore than to provide minor help from time to time? They must have known about my normal job, assuming they had been monitoring me, they must have known I was at the office from early morning until after dark, and often worked on the weekends. But reasoning didn't work with them. They weren't interested in logic, only lies.

The man with the glasses demanded I give my opinion of the many people I had worked with in the human rights movement over the years. Again, switching tactics, he offered me an out, tempting me to admit I didn't really know these people as well as I thought and that I could avoid some punishment. He tried goading me into admitting that I was just naïve and being used. He tried again to force me to say one of my partners was colluding with foreigners.

I disagreed. He was no spy, but an idealist and a truly good person. The man with the glasses dug in, attacking my naiveté, explaining that not all Chinese love their motherland, that there are many turncoats and troublemakers, that I was being played, I was too stupid to realize that a friend of mine was a spy in league with hostile foreign forces.

The next day, the guards made me sign a paper that said my detention was being extended. I had to hold the form close to my weak eyes in order to read it. The guard seemed to delight in my discomfort. "Did you seriously think that we would be done after having just held you for two days? We can keep you here legally forever."

After I had signed the forms, they launched in with the same questions as the previous day. Nauseating in repetition but the slight difference was that today they showed me some piece of "evidence," a bankcard with my name on it. They had found it in the apartment of someone I knew in the rights movement. It was supposed to have been destroyed in case we were detained.

My interrogators pressured me to confess where the money came from. I said that although of course I had seen the card before— it had my name on it—but I hadn't kept it. I had never used it and didn't know how much money was on the card, or in the bank, and I especially had no idea where the money came from or where it went.

As with the previous day, the fat man and his helper took over for the man with the glasses. The thinner of the two, the "good cop," brought me dinner.

I was so happy to eat but that feeling sank as soon as I saw I was only being given two tiny steamed buns, a small portion of cold mixed tofu strips, and a bottle of water. I hadn't eaten for well over 24 hours in captivity. I was famished and ate up my pitiful little meal like crazy. The fat man watched, deriving a sadistic pleasure from the contrast between my starved and hasty eating to the power with which he leisurely enjoyed a cigarette.

As soon as the interrogation began, he was as impatient as before, saying I was refusing to cooperate. Yesterday's horrible scene played out again in my mind, but this time I was more prepared. Again, he took me to the toilet and beat me, only for me to be saved by the thin man again. I decided this was their routine, the way they worked together. What a twisted duo.

I was exhausted from having been subjected to over 24 hours of interrogation. And since I hadn't been able to sleep properly the few days before I was taken, I was suffering from real sleep deprivation. My stomach was tight, having only had that small meal the whole time I was with them.

My mental state was slipping away. I could feel it. When the fat man was beating me, everything went into slow motion before my eyes. As he yelled at me it sounded like a voice from a very long distance away. I was so disoriented by the second night I couldn't even remember if I was beaten once or twice or if I had tried to resist. I couldn't even remember if I had screamed out in pain or not.

It was 6 on the third morning before they allowed me to sleep. I saw the clock, which is how I know what time it was. But they didn't let me sleep long, only two hours and then they jolted me awake and hurried me back into the interrogation room. Again, it was the turn of the man with the glasses.

I didn't admit to anything, but kept trying to point out that everything I had done was perfectly legal. I was just helping China develop the rule of law.

He looked at me coldly, "You can't get out of here. Did you think everything would be okay after 48 hours? I am telling you we can keep you for six months under Residential Surveillance at a Designated Location; you could spend your entire life in this small cell. After that we can just switch you to criminal detention, and after that we can send you back to Residential Surveillance at a Designated Location. Don't think you will ever escape. I can make you disappear for years. Even your wife and daughter won't know where you are."

He waved the RSDL transfer document in my face to prove the threat. Not that I could really see anything, still not having been given my glasses. The thought made me shiver. That I might be arrested had dawned on me before, but the idea of RSDL? The softness of the expression, despite its true meaning, made me feel weak.

He continued in this way, still trying to get me to admit that one of my coworkers was a spy, and that I helped him commit crimes endangering state security.

With the incessant certainty of his questioning, the sleep deprivation, the physical pain of last night's beating, the threat of disappearance, I knew I was at my breaking point. A few more rounds and the idea of Residential Surveillance pushed me over the limit.

"Yes, maybe he is a spy, I don't know, I really don't know." I was just saying what he wanted. Crying, I knew it was a betrayal. Tears uncontrollably streamed down my face and salted my "confession." Maybe I was naïve, but one way or another, all I wanted was for this all to end.

Soon after, the man with the glasses disappeared for about half an hour. Once he returned, he presented another detention notice for me to sign and a list of the items they had confiscated from my house, also to sign. He went on and explained my rights. Why was he telling me my rights now?

After two days of having been starved and beaten, I was told I had the right not to be beaten and to receive regular meals. How absurd it all felt.

After signing the paper, the man with the glasses left me to chat with his assistant. The situation and mood seemed to have changed. Had they lost interest in me? I was hopeful that they had realized their mistake. I began to feel better. Maybe they were planning to transfer me to another department, but what kind of department? Anything to escape from the fat man, I thought.

The man with the glasses returned after another half an hour or so. He told me they were taking me away and made me sign a notice of release. They didn't let me keep the paper or any documents related to my detention or release though. It was as if it had never happened.

As they prepared me to leave, they put the black hood over my head again, led me through a parking lot and into a car. I could feel when we were driving but don't know for how long, maybe half an hour, maybe more. When we arrived somewhere else, they took me out of the car.

Suddenly my covered head was slammed hard onto the hood of the car. My heart raced as horrible thoughts flooded my mind, but they were only removing my handcuffs. Then they took off the black hood. I looked around and saw that we were parked in front of some restaurant but I still didn't have my glasses and struggled to see more clearly. I noticed that a few meters away from our State Security car there was a regular police car. The heavyset officer inside got out and exchanged some documents with the State Security agents. I saw he had a large black plastic bag; it had the items they had seized from my house.

The fat policeman put me into his car but not before the man with the glasses shocked me with a parting gift: a swift and forceful slap to my face. The policeman seemed surprised, or maybe it was my imagination, but he didn't say anything.

Inside the police car, I noticed a young officer sitting in the driver's seat but he never said a word to me. The fatter officer confirmed my address. I asked for my glasses back. I had been effectively blinded for over two days and nights. He returned them along with the other items they had confiscated from my house, including my daughter's iPad. I was so relieved.

I knew then that I was really free and that all this had been some kind of nightmare. In the last few moments before we had arrived for the handover, the man with the glasses had threatened me. Knowing I was blindfolded and vulnerable, he spoke loudly to ensure I heard him asking the other State Security agents if the shovel was ready. I guess he had wanted to frighten me into thinking they were taking me out somewhere beyond the mountains to bury me alive. It worked. I had remained terrified until they left, and especially when he smacked me, but now they were gone and I was on my way home, I felt truly saved.

The two policemen didn't seem too bad. They dropped me off on the street near my house as I had requested, not wanting my neighbors to see me arriving in police custody. I walked the rest of the way.

Even after everything I had endured over the previous three days—the sleep deprivation, the beatings, the mental anguish, being threatened with disappearance and death—the hardest part was the last walk home, carrying the large plastic bag with my belongings inside, thinking how I was going to explain everything to my young and impressionable child.

The pollution in Beijing was particularly bad that day, and while I was walking and staring off into the grey, polluted sky, I thought, am I free or will this cycle be repeated? Will I be taken again tomorrow, or the next day? The next time, will I really disappear?

All I could think was that whatever happened, if they come again tomorrow, or the next day, all I wanted was to get back home to my family today.

Chapter 9
Kidnapped from across the border | TANG ZHISHUN

Tang Zhishun (唐志顺), male, born 1975 in Beijing, originally trained as an engineer. He was inspired to get involved in civil rights activism after facing (and stopping) the illegal demolition of his own home. Since them, Tang has helped other victims of forced evictions on how to better protect their rights.

Police seized Tang and barefoot lawyer Xing Qingxian in Myanmar as they were helping Bao Zhuoxuan, the teenaged son of detained rights lawyer Wang Yu (Chapter 3) and Bao Longjun (Chapter 11) to flee the country. The three were forcibly brought back to China. Tang was finally released after more than a year in secret detention, first under Residential Surveillance at a Designated Location and later under criminal detention.

It was early October 2015. I was in Mongla, a small town in Myanmar, just across the border from Yunnan, when they took me.

The night before I was taken, I had become certain that I was being monitored and that someone was preparing to take us, the three of us. I was there with another man [Xing Qingxian] and a young kid [Bao Zhuoxuan], who we were escorting for his protection. I had seen a man on a red motorcycle circling us wherever we went, observing us. At dinner we knew for certain that we weren't safe. As the motorcycle circled us again, the boy we were escorting and the man on the motorcycle stared at each other in a way that we knew he had been identified.

The next morning, while we were having breakfast at a local farmer's market, a large group of police officers arrived. As we were led away to a local police station, I noticed army personnel scattered around the market. The interrogation at the station was brief. We were handcuffed, and driven back into China. Once I had been placed in the new detention center in China it became clear the policeman in Myanmar who had interrogated us at first was not in fact local, but a Chinese officer.

On 20 October, I was picked up at the Menghai County Detention Center, a small Chinese town close to the border with Myanmar and Laos. Five policemen, three from the far northern metropolis of Tianjin, and two local officers, came and took me. First, they brought me to a small market, bought me clothes, shoes and socks, and told me to change. Once we arrived at a nearby airport, the two local police officers left.

At this point, because I had not had access to the medicine I take for hyperthyroidism for a long time, I could barely walk. My heart was racing, my body was weak, and I kept trembling all over. I was really sick.

The Tianjin policemen made me wear a hat, facemask, and sunglasses so that the people in the airport wouldn't see how bad I was. The handcuffs I was wearing were hidden under a piece of cloth. I was in such a bad state that I couldn't even make it on my own across the tarmac to the plane, and I was getting worse. They arranged for me to be driven out to the plane sitting on the luggage cart.

As we landed in Kunming, the capital of Yunnan province, I heard over the loudspeaker that the plane was flying on to Tianjin. I asked the policeman next to me where we were going. He said they couldn't get tickets to Beijing, so we were going first to Tianjin, and would then drive on to Beijing. I didn't believe one bit of it, but I kept quiet.

It was midnight by the time we arrived in Tianjin. I was brought out of the plane and through airport security to a large group of waiting police and vehicles. They put me into one of the cars.

The place they took me next would become my home for the next six months, but I had no idea where it was really located, since they blindfolded me as soon as I got into the car.

When I arrived at the secret prison, I looked around and thought to myself, "Wow, this is some fancy stuff; they are treating me like some high-level spy or something." The room was perhaps 15sqm, with its own shower and bathroom. All the walls were padded, to prevent self-harm or suicide. Even the sides of the sink, and the shower nozzle, were covered in soft material. The room had five cameras, covering the bathroom, the bathroom door, one by the bed and two more surveying the rest of the room. There was an air conditioner, a bed, and two soft round chairs next to a small table. Finally, there was a strange looking round stool. I didn't know what it was, but I would later come to learn its purpose. They called it a "criminal's stool," for my kind of "criminal."

"No talking!" "No moving without permission!" "Raise your hand if you want to say anything!" "Sleep with your clothes on!" "Put your hands on top of the blanket!" "Don't put your hands inside the blanket!" "Don't sleep on your stomach!" "Don't sleep on your side!"

All the policemen and the guards were in plainclothes.

They informed me that they would give me a blood check the next morning, so I would not be allowed to have any breakfast. They had prepared some clothes for me to change into. Three guards remained, watching, and then I was ordered to go to sleep.

The next morning, after checking my blood, and giving me some medicine for my hyperthyroidism, I was told to sit on the "criminal's chair." I was not allowed to move. It was then that I realized the windows in the cell were covered by a frosty film that blocked anyone from seeing in or out. The closed windows also had iron bars across them.

When I was forced to sit on the "criminal's chair," more of a stool really, I discovered its purpose. It was small but tall. The seat was very narrow and your legs barely touched the ground, ensuring that your body weight is focused on the small round seat. At first, for short periods, it wasn't anything I couldn't handle. But after being forced to sit for hours, I started to really feel the pain and soreness in my back and spine.

Over the coming days, I would have three interrogation sessions a day—morning, afternoon, and evening. The questions were quite interesting. They asked about things big and small. They asked about the same things over and over again; it felt like they asked me like a million times. They asked about my experiences, my work, my online commentary, the incident that landed me in the hands of police in the first place, as well as more general things such as the 4 June Tiananmen Massacre, Liu Xiaobo, the Nobel Laureate who died in custody, the Falun Gong religion, and the current crackdown on lawyers.

They also focused on some articles I had written. They even printed them out and made me sign my name on them to acknowledge my authorship. Two in particular were of special concern: *How to fight for the right of expression online*[1] and *Thirty-six strategies for resisting illegal demolition*[2].

During the interrogation sessions, if I didn't say what they wanted to hear, they would punish me. For example, they might not allow me to blink my eyes. They might force me to sit for long periods on the criminal's chair, or force me to stand in my cell for the whole day, even when I was too weak to stand and would repeatedly fall down. But, far worse than the physical mistreatment was the mental anguish I suffered.

At times they warned me that my wife and child, despite being in the United States, were not as safe as I might think they were. They could still kill them. They said the same about my mother and sister. All I owned, holdings, money, valuables, they could take everything.

At one point, they informed me that the charge against me had been changed, from illegally crossing a national border to inciting subversion of state power. What a threat! They really overestimated me.

They often wouldn't allow me to sit down in my cell. I had to stand. I would get up at 6 in the morning, and unless taken to interrogation, they made me stand throughout the whole day until it was time to sleep. The only break I got from standing would be for the five minutes they gave me to eat. They also cut the amount of food I was given in half.

Hyperthyroidism attacks would make me keel over in pain, unable to stand. Two guards would have to pick me up and hold me, just so that I would be upright. Every day, by the evening, my feet and legs would be swollen.

The torturous long periods of being forced to stand, even if guards were needed to hold me up, continued until a doctor intervened. Only then was I finally allowed to sit down.

I was told some people were beaten so badly that they had shit themselves. They told me, they could use any number of "tricks" on me. Unafraid, I told them I knew they had all the power. I accepted there wasn't anything they couldn't do if they wanted. I told them that once I arrived in this secret prison, I no longer assumed I would get out alive. "Use any trick you want," I said defiantly.

I told them a story from my past. Some years ago, I had acute appendicitis. It was so bad that it led to an intestinal perforation. I held out for 24 hours before I eventually got on my motorcycle and drove myself to a hospital. Once there, I did the hospital registration without assistance. The doctor saw my condition and scolded me, saying I wasn't "human." The four-hour operation wasn't the end of it either. An infection kept the wound from healing. They had to use scissors and a bamboo knife to clean up after the initial operation, without any anesthetic, using salt water and alcohol. It took another hour, or more. I was fully awake the whole time, joking with the doctor. After finishing the story, I told my interrogators, "If you think you can punish me worse than that, I respect you!"

They had done a thorough investigation into my background. They came to believe that I was telling them the truth, that I wasn't lying or exaggerating. During the interrogation sessions they wouldn't necessarily comment on what I said, but they would merely respond by telling me to, "think about how to survive."

They gave me a paper on which to write my confession, to admit and atone for my mistakes. Instead, I decided I would write a will, arranging for my family members, dividing property. I even included financial compensation for the police and guards who treated me decently and took care of me. As I gave it back to them, I told them I would give RMB100,000 [~USD15,000] to the person who delivered it to my family. Writing it was the first time I ever thought about my own will and testament, and it made me truly aware of death. My eyes filled with tears.

My hyperthyroidism was very serious at that time. It would sometimes feel like my heart was going to jump out of my body. My belly would shake along with my heartbeat; my whole body trembled. I felt like I was dying. Others who saw me might have thought it was because I was scared, but this was the real reason my body behaved in this way.

One of the interrogators had a family member with the same condition, and could see I wasn't faking it but was really in serious pain. They arranged for what looked like specialists to come to my cell and perform tests, a full checkup and an ultrasonography scan. They found nodules on both sides of my thyroid; one was 6cm in diameter. They also found a tumor on my thyroid. "How is this old body holding up?" I was joking with them as they did their tests. "Will you be able to sell my organs?" One specialist thought I was being surprisingly cheerful to be making jokes in a situation like this. They suggested either taking out the thyroid or something more conservative to avoid stimulating the tumor. They asked what I thought was best. I knew my opinion didn't really mean anything to them. I said I didn't care.

It did some good. They decided to increase my medication, and to try some different combinations. I would be given 11 pills in the morning, eight or nine in the afternoon, and they even started giving me three sleeping pills at night, to counter my insomnia.

Despite this, some of the guards would kick my bed, or stomp loudly next to it at night while I was sleeping, just to show how powerful they were. It really pissed me off. I told one of them that if this behavior did not kill me, once I was free, I would spend RMB50,000 [~USD7,500] to make sure someone found them and took their knees out. The little guard scoffed, "How could you find me?" I told him, "If I said I would find you in three days, I'd be exaggerating, but if I'd definitely find you in three months."

I informed the leader of the interrogation team about this mistreatment. They must have thought it was important because the stupid guard was punished; he was forced to stand for 16 hours. It was a small comfort.

Sometimes the guards would tell me my eyes were not open wide enough, and if I didn't open them wider then they would pry my eyelids apart and use a stick to keep them open. All I could say was that these were the eyes my parents had given me and I couldn't control having small eyes. On top of that, I could not see well, as they had taken my glasses from me at very beginning. "If you have the power to allow me to be re-born," I told them, "I would be happy if you could give me another body." I assumed the stupid guard who was monitoring me must have felt intense hatred toward me and just wanted to cause me as much pain as he could. Of course, he couldn't do anything without an order from his superiors. I pushed back against some of his abuse, and eventually the guard started harassing me less. I was so happy to gain a little peace.

I learned early, during questioning, after maybe half a month of being stubborn, that I was succeeding only at making myself fatigued. I learned it was better to appear to be reasonable rather than try to appear to be tough.

They started showing evidence to counter things they thought I believed, such as a video of the raid on the Bao family, who I had been trying to help, and which had led to my own detention. I told them they could ask me some questions, and I could tell them what I knew. I even told them my bank account password to convince them I was being truthful.

They appeared to believe me. But they told me it was not their decision to make. Their boss would decide whether or not to continue my interrogations and abuse. I told them I knew it didn't matter, that so many people die in this country because of injustice, and adding me to that list wouldn't make much difference.

They weren't all bad. One policeman treated me fairly well and seemed to have a kind of conscience. By then I had been inside a long time, months I think, and I asked if he could take my bankcard and take out money to pay my credit card bills. After several months of being disappeared, I was worried I would have lost a lot of money in bills and fines, and my credit score would be down. It would be good to take care of it as soon as possible. I gave him the PIN code and you know what, he actually went and paid my bills for me.

Later, the interrogations largely came to an end. Instead, the days were filled with endless custody and being forced to stay in solitary confinement in my cell, with nothing to break up the monotony.

The days without interrogations progressed the same, on repeat. Twice a day take medicine, three meals a day, allowed to nap after lunch and to sleep at night. They treated me better, or at least they were not as intent on abusing me. I was allowed to move around, walk around the cell a little. I thought that maybe they now believed I had been wrongfully placed here, but my rationality told me that was impossible. More likely, I had grown to appear useless to them, or harmless. They cut back the budget they spent on me. What used to be three or four guards monitoring me inside the cell, 24 hours a day, was cut down to two.

Still, the two remaining guards continued to watch me intently as I went to the toilet, or for a shower when that was allowed. If it had continued much longer than it did, I think I would have gone crazy; the loneliness was overbearing.

Over the course of my life, I think I must have read at least 4,000 books, and at those moments of extreme loneliness in my cell, when my mental state was far worse than any physical pain they could have inflicted, I spent time contemplating those books and their ideas. These moments also made me think about god. Could all this suffering be part of some master plan, a way to test me, to train me or force me to grow?

I didn't need to find someone to blame, but I felt strong hatred against the system for disappearing and incarcerating me. But outwardly, maybe I acted too calmly. Somehow, I smiled a lot. The guards watching me often had an expression like they thought I had gone insane, as I sat there smiling to myself in my cell.

Throughout this period, some people, psychologists, came to visit me. They wanted to guide my feelings, shape my mentality, sort of brainwash me, but they failed, repeatedly. The sense of peace I developed brought some good things.

A policeman asked if I had any requests. I told him I wanted a book to read. It would be good if he could find me an English study book—that way I'd be fine staying in here for a long time. Why not improve my English while I am a prisoner? I thought. The policeman agreed, but the bosses did not. I was given some recipe books and one geography magazine instead. It was better than nothing.

This policeman did something else that helped me. At one point, he used an expression, an idiom, when speaking to me. *Kanpo bu shuopo* (看破不说破), he said, which roughly means to be able to see the truth but not always feel it necessary to speak out. Basically, know when to keep your mouth shut. It was something I had never been good at; it wasn't my style. But perhaps it was time for me to change my style.

Toward the end, some of the guards started to talk to me more casually, and would even ask for my advice. One policeman who brought the food to my cell wanted to talk once every few days. We spoke about tea and later he brought some tea from his hometown for me to taste. Not having had tea for months, the freshness and bitterness made me so happy. In return, I offered my advice that his character and personal qualities were not suited to be a policeman in a country like China, and that he should find a new path. I explained how problems would be blamed on him, while others would take any credit for the good things he did. So if he remained being a policeman, he would eventually lose out. He became quite emotional about it as we talked. We had several talks like this one over tea.

One day, a person from the interrogation team came into my cell. He told me to write a letter rejecting the lawyer my family had hired to represent me. "We know each other now," he told me. "So let me tell you, if you insist on meeting with this lawyer, we will just take him away." I knew they could do that, so I said I could write such a letter, but that I still wanted to hire my own lawyer. They promised me that I would have the chance to meet with a lawyer, but only one designated by the state. Any power of attorney documents I wrote would only be recognized if they were for a lawyer chosen by them. I insisted that I wanted to choose my own lawyer, someone I could trust, and hire them myself. He just repeated that any lawyer I selected would only be taken away, disappeared. So I told them, okay, "I will write down the names of lawyers and you can go take them away!" They reprimanded me and told me not to be smart, blankly rejecting my humor. "You can't use us to take someone you want away!" He understood what I was doing. I complemented him.

Several days later, the interrogation team came and asked me to sign some papers saying that I accepted the state designated lawyer, a man called Dong Yang. I did what they asked.

I only met the lawyer they had forced on me once, after I had been sent to the detention center, accompanied by the interrogators. I never heard from him again.

They were continuing to decrease the medicine they were giving me. I knew I was not far from being transferred away from Residential Surveillance at a Designated Location (RSDL). When the time came, they put a black hood over my head and moved me to a regular detention center, the Tianjin Second Detention Center.

As I was being moved and we were on our way, one of the interrogators told me they had given me a new name and would use it to register me in the detention center. It is for my own good, they claimed. Their excuse was that it would make sure I didn't get a criminal record in my real name. Of course, it also meant that no one, my family, my previous lawyer, friends, not even the state prosecutor, would know how to find me. I wouldn't exist inside the detention center. They cared so much about me. I didn't bother to say anything. I will have to remember to greet their forefathers to show my appreciation.

It was 4 May 2016 when I was taken to the detention center; I spotted a calendar inside. I had been kept in RSDL, i.e. secret and solitary confinement, for six and a half months, longer than the maximum six months legally allowed under the Criminal Procedure Law. Of course, the law in China is not even as good as toilet paper. The authorities are a tragedy and a stain on humanity; the law in the country is a joke.

After I was released, some words I had once heard came back to me, expressing how I felt about the ordeal: "A place where you must come once, but never come again." Having been inside RSDL has shown me how distorted human nature can be, and what a dark place these facilities can be.

Reading books beforehand gave me lots of ideas and stories to think about and things to analyze during the endless boredom of detention. Practicing *qigong*, to be able to balance my mind, despite the oppressive loneliness, these things all helped. I think an important lesson I learned is to never lie during interrogations. One lie will require a thousand more to cover it up. You need to learn how to speak without lying but of course without revealing everything. It is important to keep sensitive information from your interrogators, without needing to lie. I strongly advise anyone at risk of detention and interrogation to practice this in advance.

The policemen would say they held no personal grudge against me, but they acted with such cruelty, tortured me the way they did, as if knowing it was not personal would somehow change anything. I believe justice comes for everyone, one day, and those who have done wrong will get the punishment they deserve.

Chapter 10
Like a lamb protesting the wolf | SUI MUQING

Sui Muqing (隋牧青), male, born 1968 in northern Jilin province, has been a practicing lawyer since the 1990s. In 2012, he began taking on rights defense cases in Guangdong. He is well known for his work defending other rights activists, including fellow human rights lawyer Guo Feixiong [Which is the pen name for Yang Maodong]. The authorities have subjected Sui to repeated attacks, including fines and beatings, because of his work on politically sensitive cases. He was also swept up in the "709 Crackdown" in the summer of 2015 and placed under Residential Surveillance at a Designated Location (RSDL).

Sui was eventually released on 6 January 2016. Unlike many other victims of RSDL, Sui has continued his human rights work. In 2017, he represented two prominent rights activists, Huang Qi, founder of human rights news website, 64 Tianwang, and Chen Yunfei, a well-known rights blogger.

It was around 11pm on 10 July 2015 when I received a Telegram message from lawyer Liu Zhengqing. He told me that the authorities had been calling lawyers in for questioning, asking them to promise not to get involved in the cases of [human rights lawyers] Wang Yu (Chapter 3), Zhou Shifeng, and Li Heping; to keep quiet. The situation was critical. He advised me to be careful.

I had heard about their detentions the day before, and had accepted an interview with Radio Free Asia, in which I had criticized the government's attack on human rights lawyers. As a lawyer myself who had always been monitored closely, although I too felt the danger, I was not aware that this time around the authority's attack would be so far ranging.

Right after I had finished speaking with Liu Zhengqing, the security guard of my building tricked me into going downstairs by saying that my car had been in an accident. My family was already asleep and so I went downstairs alone.

Suddenly, a large number of policemen appeared like thieves. I was so angry. In my opinion, this kind of trick to catch someone in the night is normally only applied to terrorists and other criminals, but today they used it on an unarmed lawyer whose only crime was words. Despicable!

A little physical altercation ensued because I asked them to show me their IDs. This was the first time I saw Domestic Security officers in uniform arrest someone. I thought perhaps that they were used to giving orders and having people obey out of fear. They didn't know that a human rights lawyer wouldn't be afraid of those wearing tiger skin.

I was taken to a local police station for interrogation. I was very tired and sleepy.

They asked if I had accepted any interviews with foreign media and if I had commented about Wang Yu and Zhou Shifeng. I told them I had. They asked me what I thought about the situation. "It is political persecution." I told them Wang Yu is a dedicated professional, righteous, and has a good reputation. What state media has done to her is slander. Zhou Shifeng, I continued, is public-spirited, hospitable;

his way of thinking is well within the law, but he wants to build a platform to communicate both inside and outside of the Party's control.

The officers explained, according to orders from Beijing, I was not allowed to do anything related to Wang Yu and Zhou Shifeng. One side of me questioned this as illegal; the other side yielded power to the one holding the gun. I agreed that I would not comment any more until the state officially published news of the situation.

The Domestic Security officers then told me to write a note promising that I would not comment or make any other statements. This was the bottom line. I had already agreed and signed my name on their document, but now they were asking me to write a note as well. I considered it too humiliating. I refused.

Over the years, friends and the media have questioned why I became a human rights lawyer. I have always considered that there are three reasons. First, it is about holding on to my personal dignity and rights; second, my hope that my child will be proud of me in the future because I hadn't just drifted along when I was young; and third, to advance the rule of law and better society. Always my dignity and rights were in first place, and I have had to pay the corresponding price on occasion.

Two high-level provincial police officers came to talk with me, though it was more of an arrogant lecture. One criticized me for my work, my appearance, my clothes, and berated me, saying I should study and understand the constitution, which, he explained, holds that the Communist Party rules and controls everything in the country.

Their criticisms were just the same kinds of things *wumao* [online commentators paid to "guide public opinion" by the government] had used to attack and defame me online in recent years.

Although I thought some of their opinions were reasonable, I refuted them statement by statement, and pointed out their shameful behavior of tricking a lawyer in the middle of the night. In the end, we parted on bad terms.

I was kept in the police station interrogation room until 8pm the following day. I was waiting for an arrest decision that I could never have expected; they were holding me on charges of inciting subversion of state power. I was to be placed under Residential Surveillance at a Designated Location (RSDL), which in international law really just means an enforced disappearance.

The moment they announced the RSDL decision, the police placed me in handcuffs. They started videoing me. Perhaps I had seen and heard of too many evil things in China. I had an expressionless face. Part of me wanted to say something in protest, but I knew it would be useless, like the lamb protesting the wolf's ferocity. It was pointless.

I was placed inside the Guangzhou Police Training Center, a place specifically designed for political prisoners, known as Guangdong's "Qincheng Prison" [a maximum-security prison outside Beijing known for housing high-profile purged politicians and political prisoners]. Many Chinese activists from the south, Tang Jingling, Liu Shihui (Chapter 2) and other "reactionaries" have been held here, for three to six months, released only after they confessed.

It was quite funny, the place is not far from my house and I had visited it in earlier years, at the time not knowing it was a den of horror used for persecuting activists.

I was held on the fourth floor. The doors to the corridors on the third and fourth floors were locked. Only investigators and guards were allowed to enter, while others were required to obtain permission from senior level police officers.

My daily food was the same that the guards and police got, packaged food. I was served on time and always a fixed amount. It seems that torture in different places in China is run differently. I have never heard of torture by food deprivation in Guangzhou.

Admittedly, my treatment was not as strict as other "709" victims. Sometimes a guard would interrupt me from sitting or lying but after I told them off a few times they didn't bother me that way anymore. But I still never had any privacy. The door to the bathroom and shower was always left open so they could monitor me.

For the first few days, I was allowed to read. I could read and not think about anything else. I read Hayek's *Law, Legislation and Liberty*. Normally I wouldn't be able to finish it in one year on the outside, but I finished it in one week while I was there. But the good days when I could read ended quickly. Perhaps this was also a way to make me suffer. The place was totally cut off from the outside world. There was no TV, no newspapers, or any other way to get information, so they would let you taste some joy by reading a book quietly and then take that away from you.

Each day, 12 people were divided into three teams to keep me under 24-hour monitoring. Two guards watched me inside the room; another two Domestic Security police monitored me through cameras in the next room. Another two rooms on my floor were assigned for the police and guards to rest. The room was hotel style, with three beds, about 30sqm, quite big, but the facility was a bit old. On the wall opposite the bed were two big cameras, one on the left, and one on the right. It was like the eyes of "Big Brother" in *1984*. Any small action I took would not escape Big Brother's eyes.

Not long after I was questioned, I started to think about ways of killing myself. The methods I thought about were cutting my wrists or bashing my head on the windowsill. But I need to explain. This was just a kind of mental preparation, kind of a way to escape the fear and pressure rather than building up any courage to actually do something.

My exhausting interrogations continued for about one month. Their questions were very detailed and wide-ranging. They touched on all the meetings I had attended with other rights defenders since 2012, every human rights case that I had defended and my fees. They focused on my links with foreign diplomats and other politically sensitive people, any trainings and meetings I had attended outside China, and other similar things. I had forgotten most of the details, especially those that weren't related to my casework, so I couldn't answer many of their questions.

Two of the things they really focused on in the interrogations were my interactions with [human rights lawyer] Guo Feixiong and the human rights cases that I had been involved with that had had a bigger impact. To be honest, because of my personal interests and difficulties in jumping over the wall [to bypass China's Great Firewall with a VPN, etc.], I didn't know that many famous rights defenders.

I had known Guo Feixiong for a long time and kept in touch with him because I admired his knowledge, character, and both of us agreed on many issues. After he was taken [Guo's arrest on 13 August 2013], the media started paying him a lot of attention, and I got to know more about him. And now with my experiences under "709", I feel that I have come to know him even deeper.

Guo had been given a nickname, "the Bear," by the Domestic Security police, because of his tough and uncooperative nature. For more than a decade, Guo has been one of the Party's main enemies. No wonder they cared so much about my relationship with him.

Perhaps I had been too busy handling individual cases that I hadn't had the time and energy to keep up with the changing political situation. I hadn't realized the obvious danger of the 709 Crackdown. Privately, many friends had warned me to be careful, but optimistically I thought they were being overly cautious. I only represented a few human rights cases. I didn't want or have the energy to get involved with other political activities. I felt safe in that I lacked the qualifications that had led to others being attacked. However the reality soon put paid to such optimism.

Before the 709 Crackdown, I had once accepted a lawyer's power of attorney who was worried about being taken. I was joking, that the more people taken the better, at least I could get more business. Who knew that in the end nothing happened to the lawyer who had designated me, instead I had to designate a lawyer for my own defense.

The investigator laughed at me, saying I should have been more aware after Guo Feixiong and Tang Jingling [another human rights lawyer] were taken. There was no one left in Guangzhou to protect me anymore.

The two Domestic Security police who were handling my case were police stars who had also handled Guo and Tang before. One of them claimed that he had read all the articles on Weibo and Twitter that I had posted, and thought my expression seemed gentle but malicious. I took it as a compliment.

Their interrogations into my other cases were aimed at making me out to be "disrupting court order" and "intentionally hyping up cases." But what they called disrupting court order was actually just me protesting against the judge for taking the prosecutor's side and rudely suppressing the lawyer. What they considered intentionally hyping up cases was just me exposing the truth behind the case and related laws and regulations. None of it violated the law.

The ethics I try to follow is what Aristotle called mesotes. Mesotes values realism; Aristotle provided a very visual explanation, placing courage in the center of the three qualities of courage, cowardliness, and brashness, and that the philosophy of mesotes is about having ideals but being realistic. It means doing the right thing.

Perhaps the Domestic Security police thought I was being uncooperative, or they wanted to find a quick way to end their investigation. Around the middle of August, they suddenly started interrogating me nonstop without allowing me to sleep. After four or five days and nights like this, my body was exhausted.

At first, I didn't worry too much about this kind of torture. In the beginning, they brought in a spotlight to prevent me from sleeping. When they turned on the light I had a strange impulse. Suddenly I started staring directly into the spotlight; I saw so many colors in my eyes. The police turned it off and told me that if I stared directly into it for more than 10 or 20 seconds, I would go blind. Afterward, they didn't use the spotlight on me again.

I normally have a hard time falling asleep quickly, so I thought I could adapt to sleep deprivation torture. Although I had short rests during the gaps between interrogations, even if I closed my eyes I didn't feel like sleeping.

The torture of sleep deprivation doesn't sound that bad, but in reality it is more harmful than a lot of physical punishment and doesn't leave a trace. I remembered that I had read about Teng Biao's treatment during the Jasmine Revolution. He was often made to kneel for protracted periods and slapped about during his 70 days of detention. If I could change places with him then, I was more than willing to suffer this kind of humiliation than suffer sleep deprivation.

Early on the fifth or sixth morning of sleep deprivation, the tiredness started to hit me. My consciousness felt vague, followed by a pain I felt all over my body. It was like being roasted by a fire, while at the same time feeling extremely cold. It was a kind of pain that I had never experienced before. Faintly, I felt that I was dying.

I had previously published a post online about a Beijing poet Wang Zang, who I had once represented. The authorities had taken him because of his support for the Hong Kong pro-democracy protests; he was tortured with sleep deprivation for many days, causing the 29-year old Wang to have a heart attack. He had no history of heart disease. I was tortured the same as Wang Zang and even though he recovered, I am almost 20 years older than him. When I look back, I feel even more scared. Wang had a heart attack; I could have died. Living in a totalitarian state, the Domestic Security police responsible for the torture would at most have been lightly disciplined.

I felt the pain of roasting on a fire the whole day. From the moment I woke up, every joint and muscle was painful. It continued for almost one week, before my body was almost restored to normal.

Once I had recovered, the police finally told me the purpose of the torture: they wanted me to confess. If I didn't confess, they threatened to bind me in handcuffs and hang me from the window railing. It is said even the strongest person can only hold on for five minutes. If I confessed, I would be released. After some deep thought, I chose to confess. This meant writing my confession and recording a video, based on the instructions from the Domestic Security police.

The wanted me to say Guo Feixiong's "peaceful transition" concept was intended to subvert the Party's leadership, and that, like Guo Feixiong, I had incited subversion of state power. The actions I had taken during the trial of two people I had represented [Ding Jiaxi and Liu Zhou] had challenged the judge, who was a Party member, and were intended to defame the Party and incite subversion of state power.

I wrote a self-criticism letter. I heavily criticized my mistaken understanding. The Communist Party had created the constitution and the law. The Party is above both, and not subject to their restrictions. I shouldn't have believed that the Party should have to operate according to the law; that it would have to be under the supervision of the people. I was misdirected.

About the forced confession: In the beginning I felt very humiliated, just like many other people. But I soon changed the way I thought. I tried my best to maintain my own conscience's bottom line. I didn't say anything that would incriminate others or endanger others. I was helpless to resist the powerful regime. Although I didn't have the power to protect my dignity, at least I didn't hurt others, so I felt no qualms in the end.

Thinking about it afterwards, the authorities had actually inadvertently raised my profile. They gave me such a noble crime, "inciting subversion of state power." I was just handling individual cases, but from what the police said it seems I didn't even know I had such a noble purpose. Although it was a forced confession, it looked like I was accepting an award. Activist Chen Yunfei always lamented that he didn't get a certificate of merit for "subversion of state power." But I'm not sure whether this is a reward or a suffering from god. Maybe both.

After I delivered my confession, sometimes I wouldn't see the investigators for days on end. I felt extremely bored because I could only sit in the room and daydream. Once, a police officer inadvertently left two pages of newspaper behind. I could recite almost everything on those pages, even the advertisements.

The days were boring, but the pain of missing my family was the worst suffering.

The day before I was taken, I had been arranging for my father, who was nearly 80 years old, to be hospitalized in Beijing. I didn't know at that time how his health was holding up. I was very worried that the same thing that happened to Tang Jingling's mother, who died while he was in prison, could happen to my father. It was the first time that I hadn't seen my wife and son for such a long time. I especially missed my lovely son. When I thought about this, I felt even more terrible. I thought I was going crazy. I thought about it after I was released.

Perhaps the Domestic Security police didn't need to torture me, they could have just locked me up without any connection with the outside for two to three months, and I would have surrendered and confessed by myself.

By the end of October, three months after being taken, I was allowed to read books again. This was the best thing about my last month of detention. I read more than a dozen books on theory, such as *Commentaries on the Laws of England* by William Blackstone, *Two Treatises of Government* by John Locke, and *The Open Society and its Enemies* by Karl Popper. Outside, in freedom, books like these would take a long time for me to read; inside in detention, I raced through them.

I really wanted to carefully read the Holy Bible. I am ashamed to say that although I believe in God and have been going to church since 2004, I have never been baptized or read the Holy Bible all the way through. God has had the biggest impact on my life philosophy, far more than the 1989 Democracy Movement. God has shaped my views of society, history, and law. Through God, I came to realize the limitations of human beings, and the importance of being calm and humble. Unfortunately, uncharitably, they refused my request for a copy of the Holy Bible. From that you can see how hostile and vigilant the authorities are in their outlook on Christianity, the Church, and the Bible.

At one point during my interrogations, they showed me a photo of me from 4 June 1989, and they asked me to explain what it showed. I had never seen this photo before. It was precious, a witness to the most unforgettable years of my youth.

Domestic Security officials also asked me to talk about the disputes inside the human rights lawyers' community. In recent years, from time to time, some people have posted defamatory things about me or spread rumors about me online, and also unrealistically raised the profile of others. The police asked, since I seemed like a person who was sharp and tough, why did I keep quiet and not respond? I said I was too busy denouncing those who abuse their power; that gave me an outlet to vent and so I had no need to care about other "noise."

The police promised to release me after three months, but I was actually held for nearly five months. They freed me on bail on 2 December 2015. In the final weeks before I was released, I was transferred to a nearby hotel. The room was much better. I could watch TV, but it was much noisier than previously. The last place had been quiet, which was good for reading. I was allowed to meet my family two to three times. I could walk around but I remember there was a few days that my legs felt week because I lacked calcium and because I had been kept without any sunshine, I couldn't walk or stand steadily.

I went into hiding for four months after the 1989 Tiananmen Square [Crackdown]. After I was caught, I spent months in prison. Perhaps then I was young and naïve but the suffering back then was much less than my experience during the 709 Crackdown. The ravaging of human rights and rule of law, still ongoing today, has symbolic significance. Perhaps it means the dream of peaceful transition is totally shattered.

When I look back, before I was taken I think I was really naïve. As an experienced lawyer, I even subconsciously believed in China's laws. I never really thought that the government would kidnap people like this. And that is what RSDL is: just plain kidnapping. How shameful!

The 709 Crackdown is an attack on the human rights movement; it follows the earlier attacks on the New Citizens Movement[1] and Southern Civil Rights Movement.[2] Still, I believe the 709 Crackdown is not the end of China's civil rights movement. It marks beginning of a new stage.

Chapter 11
This society eats people | **BAO LONGJUN**

Bao Longjun (包龙军), male, born 1970 in Inner Mongolia, is a long-time legal rights activist. He worked for the Feng Rui Law firm in Beijing with his wife, the rights lawyer Wang Yu (Chapter 3) and disappeared lawyer Wang Quanzhang.

Bao was one of the first to disappear in what became known as the "709 Crackdown" against rights lawyers in the summer of 2015. He was seized at Beijing airport with his teenage son before they could board a plane to Australia, where his son was planning to attend school. That same night, security agents raided his Beijing home and abducted his wife. The couple was placed separately under Residential Surveillance at a Designated Location and remained prisoners until they were finally freed more than a year later.

Ye who would know what evils man can inflict upon his fellow without reluctance, hesitation, or regret; ye who would learn the limit of human endurance, and with what bitter anguish and indignant hate, the heart may swell, and yet not burst—peruse these Memoirs.
-- Richard Hildreth, *The White Slave*

Before the "709 Crackdown" had even begun, bad omens were already predicting trouble. A month earlier, in June 2015, an article attacking my wife [Wang Yu, Chapter 3], published on an unknown website from Tianjin, went viral. The article was full of lies and vulgarities maligning my wife. Following its publication, many lawyers stood up and immediately denounced it, but the authority's intent was clear. The attack against Wang Yu had started.

I didn't imagine things would move so fast, so intensely, or so violently as they did. They started by taking me. I had never dreamed that I would be the target of their crackdown.

On 9 July 2015, I was supposed to be taking my son, Bao Zhuoxuan, to Australia where he was enrolled in high school. Our flight from Beijing was at 1am. I still wonder if our plan to go abroad made them bring forward the start of the Crackdown.

We had just collected our luggage from the security scanner and were heading toward the departure hall when five or six people moved in to block our way. None of them was in uniform.

They asked: Are you Bao Longjun? I had barely answered yes, before they rushed forward, surrounding us. The one who had asked my name dragged me by the arm. The smell of cigarette smoke clung heavily to his body. I always associate that kind of sharp smoke smell with villains. He produced some kind of notebook and waved it in front of my face as he explained they were from the Beijing Public Security Bureau. I only heard this much of what he said as I was being dragged away. At that moment, I only thought that we would be banned from leaving the country.

I was in shock. I turned my head and saw my young son being dragged by two of them as well, following right behind me. I was afraid he would miss his flight. I shouted: "He is just a kid! He has nothing to do with our work. His passport is in my pocket. I need to give it to him so he can go abroad for school."

They didn't care. We walked out of the departure hall and into chaos. I saw several police cars waiting outside, their lights flashing. Somebody was filming us. It must have looked like a scene from a movie, of a suspect being extradited from abroad. They dragged me to an SUV, pulled a black hood over my head, and slid me into the back of the car. Two people quickly got in and sat on either side of me. By then, I understood that they were not only banning me from going abroad but that they were kidnapping me.

The car set off and we left the airport. With the black hood over my head I could only vaguely discern the pale yellow street lighting but I had no idea in what direction we were traveling. I was nervous and didn't speak a word along the way. I had never experienced anything like this. I didn't know what they were going to do. I was very scared.

After we drove for a long time, the car shifted onto a small road and shortly after we finally came to a stop. They pulled me out of the car. We entered a room, and my black hood was finally removed. I looked around. It was a small place, a single bed with a blue bed cover, a table with a blue tablecloth, and an armchair also covered in blue fabric. The walls were covered in white padding. There were at least three cameras monitoring the room.

People kept coming and going; one of them ordered me to take off my clothes. I removed my T-shirt obediently. "Take it all off!" he ordered harshly. I wasn't wearing much since it was summer, and only had underwear left to remove after taking off my shorts. I looked at him meekly. "All of it!" he repeated. I was scared and immediately slid off my underwear. He pointed to the bed, saying there were clothes there for me to wear. Lifting the sheets, I saw a few articles of clothing under the pillow: a black T-shirt, underwear, socks, and navy blue shorts. A pair of slippers had been placed by the side of the bed. I quickly got dressed. As I finished, the man spoke aggressively, "Stand against the wall. You are not allowed to move!"

The People's Republic of the Disappeared

He left with my clothes. Two men entered. After moving the table to the center of the room and adjusting the two chairs beside it, one of them aggressively ordered me to stand upright. I had been leaning against the wall; I jerked my body straight. The dynamic was one of master and apprentice. This was how my first interrogation began.

I can't remember much about this session. I only vaguely recall talking about the injustices suffered by my family and asked them to return my son's luggage and passport. I remember the interrogation sessions were intermittent but that they didn't let me rest. They provided me breakfast, lunch, and dinner, but I didn't eat. The next day, after a full night of interrogations, I started to eat a little. The third night, during a gap in the interrogation, I couldn't stand it any longer and I asked the two guards if I could sleep for a while. They nodded. I fell into a deep sleep.

When I woke up I could see it was bright outside. The next time I saw the interrogators their attitude was better. They appeared to show compassion for my family, the attack against my wife, and promised they would return Bao Zhuoxuan's passport and luggage. I felt so grateful, but it was all a ruse to trick me, to lull me into a false sense of security.

They said I was under suspicion of inciting subversion of state power, and that I was being placed under Residential Surveillance at a Designated Location (RSDL). They asked me to sign my name on a notice but I refused.

Later on, another person was added to the interrogation team. He spoke with a heavy Tianjin accent. He said he was from Tianjin Public Security Bureau.

They had made a list of my confiscated belongings. I saw that my son's luggage had been taken off that list as if to prove that they were being honest when they told me that my son was safe. They said that they had returned his stuff and that none of this would affect his ability to study abroad. It wasn't until later that I understood it was all part of their trick.

They focused their interrogations on my interactions with more than 20 lawyers and activists. These included a Beijing workshop on Fan Mugen's case, who was one of my wife's clients; the Jiansanjiang incident[1] and the dinner we had held for Wang Quanzhang's return after he was beaten in Jiansanjiang; a training in Thailand; details about the Fengrui Law Firm, and others. I answered some questions truthfully but concealed some information so that I could avoid incriminating others.

It wasn't until much later when I had been transferred to Tianjin and was visited by state-assigned lawyers, who I also happened to know, did I realize the full extent of what was happening. The lawyers told me the list of those who had been detained. I was shocked.

There were a few matters that my interrogators seemed the most interested in. They kept coming back to these same questions again and again.

They asked about a training I had attended in Thailand. I explained it was an IT training, and that I hadn't really learned anything, and that I had mainly gone to have some fun. I told them that the manual was still in my laptop, and that they could find it if they wanted. They questioned me about that Thailand training several times and said they knew it had been organized by the so-called Anti-China force, *Weiquanwang* [Chinese Human Rights Defenders, a human rights NGO].

They asked about Fan Mugen. He was one of Wang Yu's clients, and I was the assistant. I had attended a workshop on his case, but I didn't know who had organized it. Other famous lawyers were there, including Li Heping. They asked me why Wang Yu had taken the case. I explained that local household owners had wanted her to represent him. His house was being illegally demolished in Suzhou and as he was trying to protect it from the demolition team he accidently killed two of them.

They also asked about Cao Shunli.[2] I told them that Cao Shunli had died during her arbitrary detention, before Wang Yu was properly able to represent her in court. They asked me if I knew Teng Biao (Foreword), but I didn't. They also questioned me about Ilham Tothi,[3] another of my wife's clients. I told them she only represented him during the investigation period, and that they had only met up a few times.

While I was being questioned, I could sense the danger my wife was facing, and so I pressed them to tell me about her condition. They told me she was fine, and even swore "on Mao's name" that they were telling me the truth.

They thought I was honest. I didn't resist. So they started treating me better.

I was kept in a small room with an attached bathroom. This small room was covered all over with white padding; even the sides of the toilet and sink were padded [a suicide prevention measure]. The light was on 24 hours a day. The curtain was heavy, and rarely opened.

Other than when I was being interrogated, two guards watched me 24 hours a day. Normally each team would take turns every two hours. For the first seven to eight days, they subjected me to frequent interrogations. At night, two guards watched me, even when I went to the toilet or brushed my teeth. One would stand inside the bathroom, and another by the door. One of them had a small book in his pocket. Every 10 minutes, he would take it out and make notes. My daily routine was entirely regimented, except for the interrogations. Also, every day a medic would come and take my blood pressure.

One day, an interrogator told me they were changing my location because my room was going to be renovated. They put me back in the black hood to be transferred. The trip only took a few minutes, and they drove very slowly. The new place was a big empty room, about 20sqm, and the walls were also covered in white padding. There were no windows. There were three or four cameras on the wall staring at me. Sometimes I could hear the sound of a camera moving. There was no toilet in the room. Each time I needed to use the toilet or brush my teeth I had to ask for permission. They would put a black hood over my head and two guards would take me to the toilet.

I often heard them speaking on walkie-talkies: "Number 2 is brushing his teeth;" "Number 2 is in interrogation,"etc. I came to realize that they were referring to me, that I was "Number 2." Sometimes I heard them mention other numbers and from that I believe that at least four other people were being held on my floor.

One day the door opened while the guards were changing shifts. I heard the voice of [human rights lawyer] Li Heping asking for his restraints to be loosened. I assumed he was asking the guards not to drag him too roughly while he was using the toilet. I was so happy to hear him, even though we couldn't speak; after such a long time, at least I could hear a friendly voice.

Imagine it, in this place you can't talk with anyone except your interrogators. I really hated the interrogation sessions. Whenever I heard the sound of chairs being moved, I became instantly nervous, because I didn't know what they would ask me and how I could answer in a way that wouldn't hurt others.

Although I hated the interrogation sessions, if they didn't happen for a few days, I would start to worry: Had something gone wrong? At least they were some kind of interaction, and after a few days in isolation I would hope for a chance to talk with anyone. This is what it was like. My condition? I was depressed, afraid, and lonely all the time. Each day felt like a year. Every day I dreamed about getting out of this shithole.

My interrogation sessions became less frequent once they moved me to the new location. After several days without seeing any interrogators, the interrogator from Beijing came into my room. "Old Bao," he called out. "You are going to be fine. You will be released soon."

A few days later he saw that I had washed my prison clothes and was drying them on the interrogation table. He asked me: "Why are you washing these clothes? You are going back home soon." These words became my hope. I was ecstatic at the thought of release, to be reunited with my son and wife. But day after day, a whole month passed, and there was no sign that I would be released.

Finally, after one interrogation session I asked: "Didn't you say I would be released soon?"

"The leader didn't agree to your release. What can I do?"

I was destroyed. In the following days, I would pace my cell, the guards standing a distance apart, demarcating the limits of my freedom.

As I walked between them, I thought about that line from *Notes from the Gallows* by Julius Fuchik. "Seven steps from the door to the window, seven steps from the window to the door."

But, unlike Fuchik, I wasn't allowed to reach the door, or the window. I could only walk back and forth between the two guards. Every day, I spent long hours walking like this. I was like a wolf in a cage, but I couldn't howl like a wolf, because I wasn't allowed to make a sound. If even the smallest whisper came from my lips as I recited poetry, as I often did to myself in times of extreme boredom, they would stop and reprimand me. "You're not allowed to move your lips," they would say.

I had been a prisoner in this closed and lonely environment, without books, newspapers, TV, for already 40 days at this point. I had taken to reciting all the poems I knew deep in my memory.

I missed my family the most. I wondered if my son had made it abroad? Who was taking care of my father, who had been bedridden and sick for three years? How was my mother's health? Sometimes I would ask my captors about my son, but they always gave me the same excuse—they had no idea. They would say: "Your wife is out. She will take care of him. There's no need to worry." Of course, that too was a lie.

After the first 40 days, they found something else to do. They asked me to provide the password for my phone. After they asked several times, I finally relented. I remembered clearly the night when I gave them my password, the thunder and lightning outside felt like it was going to split the building in two. Afterwards, they recovered part of my Telegram chat logs from my phone, which mainly included some information on [activist] Xue Mengcun and my support for Occupy Central [a 2014 pro-democracy movement in Hong Kong].

They wanted to know everything I had done, everything about my past, everything private, and every contact I had had with others. In their eyes, I was obliged to tell them everything about myself. I had no privacy or right to hide anything. They acted as if they had the absolute right to do this to me. They act is if they own you, as if you are just one of their animals, a pig. They can control you in whatever way

The People's Republic of the Disappeared

they want. This made me angry, but I could only curse on the inside. On the surface I had to appear obedient.

While I was detained, sometimes I would hear strange sounds. I heard a woman continuously crying for a few days. The sound was intermittent. It didn't sound real, but it made me very anxious. It sounded like Wang Yu's voice. I asked the interrogator who was crying. Was it Wang Yu? They told me that nobody was crying; that I must be hearing things. Then I heard them whispering about the sound insulation not being good enough.

One day the guards came into my room and put a black hood over my head again. I thought perhaps that I was going to be released. But after a few turns, I was just taken into another small room. It was the room where I had stayed in the beginning, the one they had to renovate.

Now the walls were no longer covered by white padding but by dark red leather. The whole place smelled pungent from the renovation. One of the guards, as if expecting congratulations, asked me, "Doesn't it look nice now?"

"These are all cells. How does it matter if they are beautiful?" I retorted.

After the transfer, my interrogators came every day for the next three days, mainly pressing me for details about my wife and Wu Gan.[4] Then they didn't come for eight or nine days.

When they came back, they tried to convince me that once I was released, I should try to persuade my wife to abandon her path. They left abruptly to let these words sink in. Somehow, I was suddenly filled with hope again.

Of course, after a few days my hope was dashed again. It was 8 September, and the Beijing interrogator came back, with a large group of people this time. He told me they were changing me to another location.

They moved me to Tianjin. I had already been detained for two months in Beijing. Now a further four months in Tianjin were about to begin.

The Tianjin room was newly renovated—it was as though they were renovating secret facilities like these all over the country—and it smelt pungent, with the same leather covering on the walls, the same bed cover and tablecloth. Everything was the same.

In Tianjin, my cell was on the first floor. I could hear the sounds of birds and people outside. But not long after they installed an iron plate over the window. They also took away my armchair and swapped it for a small round stool. It was very uncomfortable to sit on since it had no back support. The armed guards in Tianjin were stricter. They looked younger, fresher, so they followed the rules more zealously, and they were unbending. The space I could move around was much smaller than in Beijing, and they limited the amount of time I was allowed to walk in my cell.

I grew angry. "Is this Residential Surveillance? Does the law allow you to implement Residential Surveillance at a case handling location? What basis is there for you to hold me? Doesn't the law require basic evidence for a criminal act? Months have passed. What kind of criminal evidence do you have? What reason do you have to keep me?"

It was getting harder to sleep. Since I couldn't sleep in the night, I felt super tired during the day, but they never let me rest. It was also not easy to wash. They did not let me take a shower for the first half of the month that I was there. Their excuse was that there was no water. I was made to wear the same clothes I wore in Beijing. After requesting many times, they finally gave me new clothes and socks and I was able to take a shower once a week.

I became obviously thinner. Once when I was taking a shower, a guard whispered to me, "I remembered you looked muscular when you first arrived. Not any more."

You can't eat well or sleep well in that place. There was always someone staring at you. They even check to make sure you are really defecating when you go to the toilet. One guard told me that they had to make sure people weren't pretending to use the toilet in order to avoid standing all day. There was no peace.

I had to ask their permission for everything, including swallowing my own saliva. I couldn't stand all the rules. I asked to see the leader. Someone who seemed like a platoon leader came in. He said, "Asking for permission to swallow your saliva is for your own good. We are afraid that you might choke."

I often woke up from nightmares. Sometimes I would be so panicked from a bad dream that I would jump out of bed. Once, I even scared a guard.

But what hurt the most was what they did to my son.

One night, after I had been in captivity in Tianjin for over a month, I was half asleep when someone came into my room and told the guards I needed to get up for an interrogation session. I hadn't had nighttime interrogations for a long time; not since my first week in RSDL. I felt that it must be something big. I was nervous.

I asked them to bring me my clothes. At night the guard made me keep my clothes in a storage box outside the room. They had so many small rules. After I had dressed, the interrogators came into the room with the same laptop and camera that they always brought.

"Bao, didn't you always ask me for news about your son? Now we have some; good news and bad news. Which would you like to hear first?"

As soon as they said they had news about my son, I was excited that my mind became cloudy, or perhaps it was a premonition of what he was about to say. I heard snatches of him saying that my son hadn't gone to Australia, but was studying at the Number One Middle School in Ulanhot [in the Inner Mongolia region] with help from the Tianjin police. Wasn't this good news? Ulanhot Number One Middle School is very hard to enter. Shouldn't I thank the Tianjin police?

I remember saying something like, why would I want to thank the police? It was you who wouldn't let him leave to study overseas in the first place. Which is better, Melbourne or Ulanhot? Isn't it obvious? I demanded to know how they could deprive my son of his right to study abroad. Then I remembered. What was the bad news? I asked.

He said my son had been kidnapped and then smuggled into Myanmar. But local police had found him and deported him back to

China. There was an investigation. He showed me a report from Yunnan police, attached was a photo of my son.

This was the first news I had had of my son for three months. The photo was the kind taken when you enter a detention center. I had also made one under when I entered the Tianjin detention center. When I saw the photo of my son, my tears flew uncontrollably.

I cried for three full days. I missed my son so much. I held onto images of him playing with me when he was young. I dreamed of hugging him, kissing him. I swore that I would never shout at him again. I told the guard: "You don't know how kind-hearted he is. If we saw a beggar, he would always get one kuai from me and give it away." I didn't walk any more, only sat there and let my tears flow.

I sincerely doubted that my wife was "fine" like they said. I asked them: "Where is Wang Yu? Didn't she leave together with him? Who took my son?"

A few days later, they started interrogating me frequently. They asked if I knew Tang Zhishun (Chapter 10) and [activist] Xing Qingxian [the two men who were trying to help his son escape out of China]. I said I didn't.

After another seven to eight days, they brought a print out of my Telegram chat history. I told them that they could just write down the Telegram group record and I would sign it. The chat history was just about supporting friends who were taken during Occupy Central, and helping them find lawyers. They claimed that my behavior was a criminal act, receiving outside funding to endanger state security. I pointed out: 1) those who supported Occupy Central were all detained on charges of disturbing public order, which is not a crime of endangering state security; 2) any money was provided by Xue Mengchun, the deputy chief of a company, not a foreigner, so it had nothing to do with accepting foreign funding; and 3) the lawyer's fee that I helped to pay was simply for representing a client and had nothing to do with endangering state security.

Since when is representing a case endangering state security?

The guards had grown stricter. They had changed to a team of evil guards. I was not allowed to walk at all. I asked if I could stand. But they told me not to even think about sitting down again if I stood up. When I was thirsty and asked for water, the guard told me that in the future, for my health, they couldn't let me drink cold water. But they also wouldn't give me warm water to drink. I had to stay thirsty until meal times.

I still remember one thing the guards said: obedience is everything.

Soon it was December. They still hadn't found any evidence to prove my guilt. By now, I felt that they had become less strict. Sometimes a guard would open a curtain a little bit, and although a sheet of metal covered the windows, the gorgeous and beautiful sunshine couldn't be covered. The sun shined inside the room. That was freedom sunshine.

They started trying to convince me to accept a state-appointed lawyer. I told them that I wanted my own lawyer, and they asked me to suggest some names. I gave them a few, such as Fang Ping and Jun Jie. They told me that some of these lawyers had been taken too and told me not to make trouble for others. They would detain any lawyer I named.

"Do we still have the law?" I asked.

"No. The law does not apply to you," they answered.

I strongly opposed accepting one of their lawyers. I told them that I could represent myself. But it didn't make any difference. They tried to convince me every day. In the end, they almost begged me to sign. They told me, "You can see that nobody comes to this corridor anymore except us. All the others have signed. You are the only one who didn't. Once you sign, you will be able to go home."

I didn't see another way out. I told them, "I have never had any news about my wife. You guys think she might be taken like me, so can you go find out if she was taken? If she was also taken and if she signed accepting state-appointed power of attorney, then I too will sign."

They seemed very happy and left. They came back before noon and showed me a picture on their phone. It was the "application" Wang Yu had signed accepting the state-appointed lawyers. I later found out she had not signed such a document; they had completely faked it. But at the time, I thought I recognized Wang Yu's handwriting so I signed their document and accepted their lawyer. That was 5 January 2016.

Three days later, I received a notice of arrest from the Tianjin Procuratorate. In the evening I was sent to Tianjin Number 2 Detention Center. By that time, my six months of RSDL had been used up.

I always think, in determining whether a regime is cruel or not, we should look at how it treats its citizens. Political philosopher Montesquieu once wrote that the feature of an autocracy is to make the people afraid. People do love freedom, but the reason why they succumb to autocratic regimes is because there are no restrictions on power. There are no ways for redress.

Since the day Wang Yu was wrongly convicted,[5] I completely lost my confidence in this country. I gained a deeper understanding of the judicial darkness of this country. Now, in the face of these illegal acts and injustices, I don't know how to resist, because legal redress is broken. I have a clear understanding that this country has all the power, and its ruler will keep hold of this this power unscrupulously.

This is a society that eats people. It is not just, it is not fair, and it has no conscience.

Chapter 12
RSDL and Enforced Disappearances, a Legal View | MICHAEL CASTER

With invaluable contribution by lawyer You Luchen (尤陆沉) in researching, analyzing, and writing up sections on Chinese domestic law.

> *A disappearance has a doubly paralyzing impact: on the victims, frequently tortured and in constant fear for their lives, and on their families, ignorant of the fate of their loved ones, their emotions alternating between hope and despair, wondering and waiting, sometimes for years, for news that may never come. The victims are well aware that their families do not know what has become of them and that the chances are slim that anyone will come to their aid. Having been removed from the protective precinct of the law and "disappeared" from society, they are in fact deprived of all their rights and are at the mercy of their captors. Even if death is not the final outcome and the victim is eventually released from the nightmare, the physical and psychological scars of this form of dehumanization and the brutality and torture which often accompany it remain.[1]*

Enforced disappearances

Enforced disappearances are not only a grave human rights violation but also a crime under international law, and like torture the practice is strictly prohibited, without exception, regardless of circumstances.

An enforced disappearance is defined, in the International Convention for the Protection of All Persons from Enforced Disappearance (ICPED), as "the arrest, detention, abduction or any other form of deprivation of liberty by agents of the State or by persons or groups of persons acting with the authorization, support or acquiescence of the State, followed by a refusal to acknowledge the deprivation of liberty or by concealment of the fate or whereabouts of the disappeared person, which place such a person outside the protection of the law."[2]

An enforced disappearance has three constituent elements: (1) an individual is deprived of liberty against their will, (2) with the involvement, at least indirectly, of the government, (3) followed by the refusal to acknowledge the taking or to disclose the fate or whereabouts of that individual.[3] It is especially the third element that places the individual outside the protection of the law, which entails "the suspension of the enjoyment of all other human rights and freedoms of the victim and places him or her in a situation of complete defenselessness."[4]

An enforced disappearance can begin with either an illegal or initially legal detention. It does not matter if the practice is effectively legislated within national law, such as with Residential Surveillance at a Designated Location (RSDL) under the Chinese Criminal Procedure Law. The United Nations Working Group on Enforced or Involuntary Detentions (WGEID) explains, an enforced disappearance is not limited to an illegitimate deprivation of liberty.[5]

Enforced disappearances are a continuing offence as long as the fate or whereabouts of the individual remains unknown. There is no time limit, no matter how short. This means, "the act begins at the time of the abduction and extends for the whole period of time… until the State acknowledges the detention or releases information pertaining to the fate or whereabouts of the individual."[6] Therefore, as long as an individual is held in RSDL, their family has not been notified of their taking and their fate or whereabouts are concealed, whether for a weekend or the maximum six months allowed under the law, the enforced disappearance is ongoing. And, as United Nations experts note, "every minute counts when a person is put outside the protection of the law. And when a person is disappeared, every anguished minute spent by his or her relatives without news of that person is a minute too long."[7]

Victims of enforced disappearance

International law provides for a wide understanding of victims of enforced disappearance. As such, the WGEID "does not differentiate between direct and indirect victims."[8] This is in particular recognition of the anguish caused to relatives, which, states the Working Group, is "a suffering that reaches the threshold of torture."[9]

In addition to the mental anguish suffered by relatives, victimization is exacerbated when the victim of an enforced disappearance was the primary earner, thus further subjecting family members to economic difficulties. The presence of young children in the household of the disappeared, old enough to be aware of their missing parent but too young to fully comprehend the situation, likely causing childhood trauma, is not just an assault on the rights of the child but a moral outrage. Likewise, psychological torture is experienced by the disappeared individual who, as the stories in this book show, is often taunted with threats to their family to elicit fear and the acknowledgment of their total powerlessness to protect their loved ones.

But, family members of the disappeared are often not only victims. From Argentina to China, they also become rights defenders for the disappeared. As such, the WGEID has recognized the fundamental role especially played by women in "securing and advancing the rights of the disappeared persons... often at the forefront of the struggle against enforced disappearances."[10] In China, this has absolutely been the case, such as with Li Wenzu, Wang Qiaoling, Chen Guiqiu, and Jin Bianling, the wives of disappeared human rights lawyers Wang Quanzhang, Li Heping, Xie Yang, and Jiang Tianyong respectively. In so pursuing the rights of the disappeared, they become human rights defenders themselves, and as such the state has additional obligations toward them beyond those simply of being a victim.[11]

State obligations

International law dictates that states have the binding obligation not only to conduct an effective investigation of an enforced disappearance but also to prosecute and punish those responsible, and to criminalize enforced disappearances in national law. This final point is particularly important in order to prevent against future acts of enforced disappearance.

The obligation to investigate, as held in the International Covenant on Civil and Political Rights (ICCPR), notes the United Nations Human Rights Committee, carries the expectation of a prompt, thorough, and effective investigation carried out by independent and impartial bodies.[12] It is, as the International Commission of Jurists (ICJ) explains, "an international obligation, under both treaties and Customary International Law,"[13] which means it is an obligation "that the State cannot waive." [14] As a state obligation, by definition, the initiation of an investigation is not the responsibility of the disappeared person's family or lawyer.[15]

Likewise, the obligation to prosecute and punish is a state obligation that cannot be waived. The ICPED clarifies that states should hold criminally responsible anyone "who commits, orders, solicits or induces the commission of, attempts to commit, is an accomplice to or participates in an enforced disappearance." This includes superiors who knew or disregarded information clearly indicating an enforced disappearance has taken place, or who failed to prevent or repress an enforced disappearance.[16]

The ICPED calls on states to "take the necessary measures to ensure that enforced disappearances constitutes an offence under its criminal law,"[17] that is "punishable by appropriate penalties which take into account its extreme seriousness." [18] Because of the extreme seriousness of enforced disappearances, the fulfillment of the obligation to criminalize, notes the ICJ, "is not left to the discretion of the State."[19] In China, not only is there no distinct crime of enforced disappearance, but the state appears to be attempting to hide its practice of enforced disappearance behind the veneer of the law, as will be explored shortly.

Part of criminalizing enforced disappearances, arguably, extends to adopting provisions against all forms of incommunicado detention. In this sense, the Human Rights Committee calls for States to enact provisions that stipulate detainees are only held in officially recognized locations, that their names and location of detention, along with the names and official positions of those responsible for their detention, as well as the time and place of all interrogations should be recorded, and kept in effectively available public registers.[20]

Drawing on state obligations under the International Convention on the Elimination of Discrimination against Women (CEDAW), the WGEID holds that "a gender perspective should be incorporated in all measures, including legislative, administrative, judicial and others, taken by States, when dealing with enforced disappearances." This includes the "adoption of relevant legislation, provision of financial resources and establishment of national machineries addressing discrimination and promoting women's equality and empowerment."[21]

It is precisely the role of the government in the taking, and the refusal to acknowledge the deprivation of liberty and the fate or whereabouts of the person taken, that separates and elevates an enforced disappearance from other crimes such as kidnapping, and calls for its distinct criminalization. Any definition of enforced disappearance must also recognize the family members of the disappeared as victims, and provide for effective remedy to all victims.

Right to remedy, right to truth

The right to remedy is firmly established in numerous international conventions and jurisprudence,[22] and specifically in Article 24 of the ICPED, which holds that "victims of enforced disappearance have the right to obtain reparation and prompt, fair and adequate compensation," covering material and moral damages as well as other forms of reparation.[23] The Basic Principles and Guidelines on the Right to a Remedy and Reparation outlines international standards on the expanse of reparations mentioned under Article 24 of the Convention. These are: *Restitution*, to restore the victim to the original situation before the rights violation occurred, such as to restore freedom, residence, or employment; *Compensation*, to be provided for economic damages and likewise such damages as physical or mental harm, and moral damages; *Rehabilitation*, further covering physical and mental health care; *Satisfaction*, including "verification of the facts and full and public disclosure of the truth," a public apology, or filing of criminal charges against the perpetrator; and *Guarantees of non-repetition*, such as the effective criminalization of enforced disappearances and prosecution of those responsible. [24] Under the Basic Principles, states should ensure the public, and especially victims of enforced disappearance, are aware of and have effective access to their rights to such remedies.[25]

The right to truth is likewise widely recognized in international law,[26] characterized as inalienable,[27] and specifically outlined in the ICPED as "the right to know the truth regarding the circumstances of the enforced disappearance, the progress and results of the investigation and the fate of the disappeared person."[28] This is further clarified by the WGEID to include the identity of the perpetrator(s).[29] In this sense, the right to truth is related to the state's obligation to investigate and prosecute, but also to preserve archives and other evidence concerning violations of human rights and to facilitate knowledge of those violations.[30] The WGEID emphasizes that a state is required specifically to ensure measures to ensure women have knowledge and access to the procedures on how to request and obtain information.[31]

While the right to truth is linked to the freedom of expression and information, which can be restricted under limited circumstances, including "the protection of national security or of public order,"[32] the right to "know the truth of the fate and whereabouts of the disappeared person is an absolute right, not subject to any limitations... or exceptional circumstances."[33] The WGEID explains that, "the State cannot restrict the right to know the truth about the fate and the whereabouts of the disappeared as such restriction only adds to, and prolongs, the continuous torture inflicted upon the relatives."[34]

As with all gross violations of human rights, and especially concerning enforced disappearances, it is important for states to provide "appropriate and effective mechanisms for society as a whole" to know the truth.[35] In other words, the right to truth is both an individual and collective right, entitling not only each victim to the truth, "but the truth also has to be told at the level of society as a 'vital safeguard' against the recurrence of violations."[36] In China's case, this would mean not only an obligation to truth for victims of enforced disappearances but also one to provide truth on RSDL at the structural and societal level, such as the total number of cases, reported abuses, and perpetrators; however, as of now, many cases of RSDL are kept completely off the public record based on claims of 'national security' exceptions.

Enforced disappearances, other human rights violations, and crimes

Enforced disappearances violate a range of fundamental rights, including the right to liberty and security of the person, to be free from arbitrary detention; the right to a fair trial; the right to an effective remedy; the right to know the truth regarding the circumstances of a disappearance; the right to protection and assistance to the family, and the right not to be subjected to torture or other cruel, inhuman or degrading treatment or punishment.[37] Men and women experience enforced disappearances differently, and women victims "are disproportionately subject to sexual violence and exposed to suffering and humiliation."[38]

Arbitrary detention

The right to liberty and security of a person, such as the freedom from arbitrary arrest or detention, is universal. The ICCPR clarifies that, "no one shall be deprived of his liberty except on such grounds and in accordance with such procedure as are established by law." [39] But not unlike how enforced disappearance can occur regardless of whether they are the result of a legal or extralegal detention, to be arbitrary does not simply mean to be against the law. The Human Rights Committee explains that arbitrariness is to be interpreted based on "appropriateness, injustice, lack of predictability and due process of law."[40] In other words, the deprivation of liberty must be legal, but also "reasonable" and "necessary."[41] With this in mind, six months of incommunicado detention of a human rights defender can hardly be seen as reasonable or necessary, while the absence of an effective legal remedy and denial of contact with a lawyer of one's choosing violates due process of the law, amounting to an arbitrary detention. Furthermore, to meet the requirement of predictability, the law cannot be vague, as the lack of clarity opens the floodgates to police and judicial harassment, precisely as has been seen with, inter alia, 'national security' crimes in China. For many, secret and arbitrary detention under RSDL likewise violates their right to a fair trial.

Fair trial

International standards are clear that anyone arrested or detained is entitled to a court proceeding to "decide without delay on the lawfulness of his detention,"[42] known as *habeas corpus*, a universal right that must be effectively available. The Human Rights Committee specifically notes that an incommunicado detention inherently denies the individual his or her *habeas corpus* rights.[43] Everyone is entitled "to a trial within a reasonable time or to release." [44] Lengthy pre-trial detention should never be the general rule. On what constitutes a 'reasonable time,' the Human Rights Committee in part explains that claims such as a case being "under investigation," a frequent explanation offered by the Chinese state for lengthy pre-trial detention, is insufficient as a justification.[45]

Furthermore, throughout RSDL, the denial of access to a lawyer of their choosing is a further infringement on a person's right to a fair trial,[46] regardless of whether they face trial or are released on bail. The right of the detained person "to be visited by and to consult and communicate, without delay or censorship and in full confidentiality, with his legal counsel may not be suspended or restricted,"[47] except under limited circumstances. However, international standards hold that communication "with the outside world, and in particular his family or counsel, shall not be denied for more than a matter of days."[48]

Despite such internationally accepted protections, many of those who have disappeared into RSDL, even after being transferred into criminal detention, have been denied all contact with their family and legal representatives, and in cases such as Xie Yang, Wang Quanzhang, and others the state has illegally dismissed the lawyer of their choosing. In other cases, individuals have been forced to deliver confessions, which in many cases were later broadcast on Chinese television.

Forced confessions, which are increasingly common, especially under RSDL, are fundamentally troubling, in part due to their absolute disregard for the right to be presumed innocent and to receive a fair trial. The ICCPR is explicit that no one shall be "compelled to testify against himself or to confess guilt," [49] but what makes forced confessions so concerning is that they frequently originate in torture. The risk of torture is already high in a criminal justice system reliant on confessions, which is compounded by the pursuit of forced confessions, and victims of enforced disappearance and secret detention are especially at risk of torture.

Torture

Any act of enforced disappearance inflicts severe suffering on the individual and their families and violates international law, which fundamentally prohibits torture.[50] That the act itself results in anguish and suffering that constitutes torture is noted above but a different situation arises, points out the ICJ, when the formerly disappeared person reappears or remains in custody but there is evidence or testimony that he or she has been tortured.[51] This requires, continues the ICJ, separate investigations and prosecutions for both the enforced disappearance and torture, and that failure to do so, or for only one, constitutes impunity.[52]

Torture is defined in the Convention against Torture (CAT) as "any act by which severe pain or suffering, whether physical or mental is intentionally inflicted on a person for such purposes as obtaining from him or a third person information or a confession... or intimidating or coercing him or a third person..." and is perpetrated by or at the instigation or with the knowledge of the state or agents acting on its behalf.[53] While CAT concludes that such pain or suffering does not necessarily include that which arises only from lawful sanctions, such sanction must still adhere to fundamental rights or may rise to the level of torture.

Like enforced disappearances, the prohibition against torture caries explicit state obligations, including "limiting the use of incommunicado detention; ensuring that detainees are held in places officially recognized as places of detention; ensuring the names of persons responsible for their detention are kept in registers readily available and accessible to those concerned, including relatives and friends; recording the time and place of all interrogations, together with the names of those present; and granting physicians, lawyers and family members access to detainees," to ensure "any statement that is established to have been made as a result of torture shall not be invoked as evidence in any proceedings," and all alleged offender(s) are subject to criminal investigation, prosecution, and punishment.[54]

Crimes against humanity

Crimes against humanity, like the crime of genocide, owes its origin to the Nuremberg Tribunal at the end of World War II, and although initially conceived in the context of a military tribunal, today international law no longer requires armed conflict for a crime against humanity.[55] It is among the gravest breaches of human rights and international law. Because it undermines the deepest values of society,[56] "the widespread or systematic practice of enforced disappearance constitutes a crime against humanity,"[57] as defined in international law. The Rome Statute of the International Criminal Court, likewise holds that enforced disappearances may amount to a crime against humanity "when committed as part of a widespread or systematic attack directed against any civilian population, with knowledge of the attack," in other words multiple acts of enforced disappearance against civilians, in carrying out or furthering state policy to commit enforced disappearances is a crime against humanity.[58]

The ICJ explains, summarizing international jurisprudence, "widespread" refers to the large-scale nature and number of victims, while "systematic" doesn't require a high number of actions, as even one action can qualify if "committed as part of a plan, a systematic practice or policy." What matters is the level of organization and predictability.   [59]

Unsurprisingly, there are no circumstances that permit for exceptions to the prohibition against enforced disappearances, "whether a state of war or a threat of war, internal political instability or any other public emergency,"[60] and yet legislating exceptions is precisely what China has attempted with RSDL. The existence of such a predictable policy of repression toward human rights defenders, through systematic legislation, demonstrates a high degree of organization and planning.

Residential Surveillance at a Designated Location (RSDL)

"Residential Surveillance at a Designated Location," is a 'compulsory measure' under the amended 2012 Criminal Procedure Law (CPL), defined in Article 73 as:

> 1.   Residential surveillance shall be enforced in the residence of the suspect or defendant; for those without a fixed residence, it may be enforced in a designated location. When crimes of endangering state security, terrorist activities or especially serious bribery cases are suspected, and enforcement in the residence might impede the investigation, it may also be enforced in a designated location upon the approval of the people's procuratorate or public security organ at the level above. However, it must not be enforced in a detention center or special case-handling area.

> 2.   Where residential surveillance is in a designated location the person under residential surveillance's family shall be notified within 24 hours, unless there is no way to inform them.

> 3.   Apply the provisions of article 33 for suspects or defendants under residential surveillance on retention of a defender.

> 4.   The people's procuratorate supervises whether or not the decision to enforce residential surveillance and its enforcement are legal.[1]

RSDL may be imposed for a maximum period of six months.[2]

An earlier draft of the CPL originally provided in paragraph 2 that family members be notified "of the reason for and location of the residential surveillance,"[3] but this requirement was removed in the final version. This is concerning, as even without applying exceptions, as explained below, the police are only required to notify family members of the person under RSDL that they have been deprived of their liberty but are neither required to inform them of the reason nor their fate or whereabouts. Furthermore, while the earlier draft had expanded on the exceptions to notification in paragraph 2, reading, "unless there is no way to inform them or in cases involving crimes of endangering state security, terrorist activity, or major bribery, when notification has the potential to interfere with the investigation,"[4] because the same exceptions exist elsewhere the removal of this clause is effectively meaningless.

While not all RSDL rises to the level of an enforced disappearance, when the authorities exercise all the exceptions at their disposal, RSDL can constitute an enforced disappearance under international law. Furthermore, torture and other ill-treatment is common and without access to a lawyer or prosecutorial oversight, followed by investigation and prosecution, the victim is effectively denied all remedy.

RSDL is the state's attempt to normalize its history of secret detention and enforced disappearances behind the veneer of the law, but as pointed out above there are no circumstances that permit for such practices and even detention procedures initially permitted by domestic law can constitute an enforced disappearance.

Secret detention before RSDL

In March 2003, then 27-year-old migrant worker Sun Zhigang died in police custody in Guangzhou. He had been held in secret for three days under the then administrative procedure known as Custody and Repatriation, which allowed the police to hold an individual, often vagrants, petitioners, and human rights defenders, in secret. Sun Zhigang's death attracted widespread condemnation, and launched the rights defense careers of two of China's best known human rights defenders: Xu Zhiyong and Teng Biao. Responding to the rising outcry, the government abolished Custody and Repatriation the following year.

However, the state soon responded with a new system for arbitrarily detaining unwanted social and political elements in secret.

Black Jails performed the same "social stability maintenance" function as Custody and Repatriation, as far as controlling petitioners and human rights defenders were concerned, but they were entirely extrajudicial, unregulated, and had no legal basis. Held in state-owned hotels, the backs of restaurants, or psychiatric facilities, and in some cases custom-built unmarked prisons, individuals abducted into Black Jails were seldom presented with charges or told how long they would be deprived of their liberty; neither were they permitted legal representation nor were their relatives notified of their abduction.

During the 2009 Universal Periodic Review before the United Nations Human Rights Council, several international organizations and governments raised the issue of Black Jails, while China flatly denied their existence. However, since then state media was slowly allowed to report on them, and some rights defenders have even succeeded at securing compensation for the victims of arbitrary detention and torture within Black Jails.

However, in 2011, during the "Jasmine Revolution," as mentioned in the Introduction and described by Tang Jitian and Liu Shihui in this book, China expanded its reliance on secret detention and enforced disappearances. These were often carried out in Black Jails, with people placed under a manipulated form of Residential Surveillance, the effective predecessor to RSDL. Previous victims of Black Jails, since the amendment of the CPL, have likewise been subjected to disappearances under RSDL.

While Black Jails served a purpose in maintaining the equilibrium of repression and silencing of petitioners and human rights defenders that had been lost with the abolishment of Custody and Repatriation, their ongoing extrajudicial presence presented an obstacle even to China's hollow rhetoric of the rule of law. With the amended CPL, and subsequent regulations, China is attempting to legislate the same repressive functions it previously pursued outside of the law, through RSDL.

Rights under RSDL

Right to a lawyer

Paragraph 3 of Article 73 refers back to CPL Article 33 on the right to a lawyer, which holds that after the first interrogation or the beginning of compulsory measures, such as RSDL, and at any time thereafter, the suspect has the right to retain a lawyer of their choosing. It only stipulates that during the investigation phase this must be a licensed lawyer. It is furthermore the obligation of the police, after the first interrogation or beginning of compulsory measures, to inform the suspect of their right to a lawyer. [5] Once a request for legal representation has been made, the authorities must promptly convey the request.

Importantly, the law states that family members or guardians may retain legal representation on behalf of the detainee.[6] However, while the CPL requires that family members be notified within 24 hours of the imposition of RSDL, exceptions effectively strip this safeguard, and further deny the right to information and truth. Defense lawyers have also called attention to the use of "text loopholes," in that a notification of RSDL may be sent to family members by post rather than by hand delivery as would be expected, which significantly delays the period of notification, which again is only required to note that their relative has been taken but not to specify the reason or location. Such loopholes are not technically a violation but its intent can be inferred from its effect—to prolong the secrecy of detention and the suffering of family members.

Article 37 provides the right to meet with one's lawyer, and that such meetings shall be private, but lawyers must first obtain permission before being allowed to meet with their clients.[7] This in effect denies the right to a lawyer. Article 34 explains that those unable to retain legal representation out of economic hardship or other reasons, may apply for assistance, and in such cases obtain a state-sponsored lawyer,[8] but the state's refusal of the detainee's chosen lawyer without justification or forcing the detainee to accept a state-sponsored lawyer should be understood as a clear infringement on this right. Only very limited mechanisms for complaint and redress exist.

Lawyers who feel that the authorities, whether the police, procuratorate, court, or others, are obstructing their procedural rights, such as to meet with their client, have the right to appeal or complain to the procuratorate at the higher level, at which time the procuratorate shall promptly investigate and notify the "relevant organ to make corrections."[9] This is a relatively weak procedural safeguard. Even so, defense lawyers recount that it is widely disregarded.

Technically, once a lawyer, or family member, launches a *habeas corpus* complaint against a case of RSDL, the procuratorate is expected to promptly initiate an investigation into its legality. [10] However, as numerous defense lawyers have stated, this is not observed in practice. Furthermore, after release from RSDL there are no effective measures for seeking remedy in cases of torture or other abuse, as the only remedy available is for the victim or his or her lawyer to file a complaint with the procuratorate, and there the investigation effectively ends. Or worse, the reporting lawyer is him or herself targeted by the state, and even themselves placed under RSDL. This is what happened after Jiang Tianyong made public allegations that Xie Yang had been tortured under RSDL and criminal detention. Because RSDL is a matter of criminal law, civil and administrative procedures are unavailable. This includes, for example, administrative litigation, which has been used frequently in the past by rights defenders to secure compensation for arbitrary detention or torture under Black Jails or Re-Education through Labor.

"Designated Location"

Article 73, paragraph 1, implies a preference for deprivation of liberty to be carried out in the suspect's residence, which earned RSDL its initial mischaracterization as a softer form of detention. Only in extreme circumstances, such as for "endangering national security" or when it would otherwise impede the investigation, the law allows for RSDL to be carried out at an effectively undisclosed "designated location." In its 2015 review of China, the Committee against Torture expressed grave concern over this provision, taken alongside the possibility of the denial of access to a lawyer, for its likelihood of permitting incommunicado detention in undisclosed locations,[11] which as noted above increases the risk of enforced disappearances and torture and should be prohibited under domestic law.

Meanwhile there is virtually no clarity on the conditions of the "designated location," leaving much to the unregulated discretion of the police or state security. The law states that RSDL is not to be carried out in a formal detention center, [12] which removes certain, albeit limited, procedural safeguards. Additional provisions clarify that the "designated location" should contain conditions for an ordinary life and rest, which, as is clear from the stories in this book, is uniformly disregarded, and that it be separate from the interrogation location,[13] similarly ignored. Defense lawyers argue that RSDL should only be for custodial purposes while interrogations should be conducted in detention centers or other formal settings and under proper supervision. That RSDL is used for both secret custody and interrogation creates the conditions for torture.

Furthermore, RSDL is not to be carried out in "special case-handling areas,"[14] which means specifically established areas for short term criminal summons and detention inside public security bureaus. In the majority of cases, RSDL is carried out in custom built facilities, which might appear as "special case-handling areas" but are not considered as such for the purposes of implementation. Rather, they are facilities effectively outside the law, because their only legal basis is found in the provisions covering RSDL, which only provides limited to non-existent oversight and wide exceptions which deny detainees various rights expected under international law.

Oversight

The Provisions on People's Procuratorates' Oversight of Residential Surveillance at a Designated Location (Provisions) was ostensibly created in acknowledgment of the state obligation to investigate and prosecute disappearances, torture, and other abuse. The Provisions stipulate that the procuratorate shall have oversight of decisions to impose RSDL, including through meetings with the defendant, their legal representative, and family members,[1] and that they may supervise implementation, including through physical inspection of the RSDL facility and in conversations with individuals held under RSDL.[2]

Namely, the procuratorate can regularly inspect the RSDL facility, at least once a week.[3] Defense lawyers have pointed to the vocabulary, in noting what the procuratorate "may" do and not what they "must" do fails to provide safeguards and does not meet the state's obligations under international law. Indeed, while the Provisions clearly note that oversight shall include whether the rights of the individual under RSDL are being protected or whether such unlawful actions such as interrogation within the designated location or abuse is taking place.[4] None of the individuals in this book recounts having seen or spoken with procuratorate investigators, even after launching complaints or explicitly asking for the procuratorate. In some cases, issuing a complaint or requesting the procuratorate only elevated or prolonged abuse. Much of the failure to adhere to even the minimal procedural safeguards and rights protection provided under the law is due to carefully designed exceptions, noted below.

Herein lies the trap, RSDL is only to be carried out under special circumstances, such as for crimes endangering national security, but while safeguards ostensibly exist to prevent RSDL from amounting to an enforced disappearance or raising the risk of torture, there are exceptions to these safeguards under the same special circumstances that allow for RSDL in the first place. Such legal gymnastics indict a systematic level of planning behind the state's use of RSDL.

Exceptions in the law

Right to a lawyer and notification of relatives

Although the CPL provides for the right to retain and meet with a lawyer during RSDL, in practice access to a lawyer for individuals under RSDL is unheard of. Under the CPL, the right to retain and meet with a lawyer during the investigation phase for crimes of endangering national security, one of the conditional requirements for RSDL, is entirely contingent "upon the permission of the investigating organ."[5] In most cases, the investigating organ is the Public Security Bureau, i.e. the police, responsible for the detention, interrogation, and abuse of the individual in the first place, so that making the right to a lawyer contingent on the approval of the perpetrator is quite clearly an effective denial of legal representation and protection.

The CPL further holds that although the authorities are required to notify family members within 24 hours once someone is taken into custody, Article 83 provides an exception in cases of crimes of endangering national security or when "notification might impede the investigation." It is important to reiterate that both of these circumstances are listed as the conditions that specifically allow for RSDL in the first place. And even though, "after the situation that would impede investigation has passed" the authorities are to immediately inform the relatives,[6] because discretion is left to the "investigating organ," this means the police can hold someone for up to six months without giving any notice to their family because "the investigation is ongoing." And indeed, this is precisely the excuse frequently employed by the police when family members and lawyers attempt to contact those under RSDL, and even after they have been transferred to criminal detention.

That an individual under RSDL can be denied access to a lawyer, and their family members refused notification of their detention, fate, or whereabouts if doing so will impede the investigation, while at the same time state media representatives have been granted access to record forced confessions clearly illustrates the arbitrariness of the exception. It is a hollow excuse used by the state to keep someone outside the protection of the law and to prolong the suffering caused to family members.

Access to a lawyer is a fundamental check against the arbitrary exercise of state power and by definition prevents against incommunicado detention. In much the same way, even in a flawed legal system, the state's obligation to investigate torture and enforced disappearances creates the responsibility for oversight, but as with the above, even this weak safeguard, is stripped from the system of RSDL.

Oversight

According to the law, the decision to impose RSDL must be approved by the procuratorate or public security organ at the next higher level, but in practice this is merely a formality. Once RSDL has begun, the procuratorate shall supervise whether the decision to maintain RSDL and its enforcement are legal.[7] However, the power of the procuratorate to supervise is weak, as in China the police exercise more power, and as such they are essentially only empowered to issue a corrective opinion to the offending party. As noted above, the procuratorate is also required to promptly investigate complaints by the detainees' lawyer or relatives, but this is quite empty if the detainee's lawyer or relative is denied all access or information.

The already weak supervisory power of the procuratorate overseeing an RSDL facility is further weakened through exceptions within the Provisions. In Article 20, the procuratorate is obligated to monitor and act against instances "except when it is impossible to provide notice" the family is not notified within 24 hours; RSDL is imposed in a detention center, administrative jail, or other locations that are not allowed under the CPL; or when the individual under RSDL is illegally denied their right to meet or communicate with their lawyer.[8] However, the Provisions go on to note in the following Article that when inspecting RSDL activities, the procuratorate shall not impede the "ordinary conduct" of the police investigation.[9] Moving beyond the question of how a state prosecutor would interfere in a state investigation, what is most troubling is that the decision is left entirely to the police. This not only effectively denies the procuratorate the oversight ostensibly provided by law, to prevent abuse, it also denies detainees any avenue for reporting or initiating an investigation of abuse.

This is a notable contradiction to the Police Law, which holds that the police in the course of their official duties must consciously accept supervision from society and citizens.[10] There is no question that such denials of access or supervision places the individual clearly outside the protection of the law.

National Security Exceptions

The range of national security provisions under the National Security Law touches on almost every aspect of society, and indeed is this way in order to provide the state with such totalitarian reach. According to the National Security Law, national security means "the relative absence of international or domestic threats to the state's power to govern, sovereignty, unity and territorial integrity, the welfare of the people, sustainable economic and social development, and other major national interests, and the ability to ensure a continued state of security."[11] The Criminal Law, Articles 102 through 113 codify the range of crimes classified as endangering national security, the crime most commonly applied to human rights defenders being the subversion of state power or to incite subversion of state power, Article 105.[12] Additional regulations provide the police with even more vaguely defined parameters with which to justify exceptions under RSDL, such as to define the range of crimes as those stipulated in the Criminal Law and "other crimes that endanger national security," but with no further explanation.[13]

Chinese law stipulates that national security shall be maintained in accordance with the rule of law "by respecting and safeguarding human rights and protecting citizens' rights and freedoms in accordance with the law."[14] Of course, that national security exceptions are applied to cases of RSDL that specifically deny fundamental rights and protections, such exceptions, and their abusive effects, are not only a clear violation of international law but also of Chinese domestic law. This is not an oversight but a feature of the law.

Conclusion

Residential Surveillance at a Designated Location (RSDL) represents China's attempt to normalize enforced disappearances behind the veneer of the rule of law.

RSDL is only to be carried out under special circumstances, or so says the law, such as for crimes of endangering national security, but even though the law and other regulations ostensibly provide for procedural safeguards to prevent RSDL from becoming an enforced disappearance, there are exceptions to every safeguard permitted under the same special circumstances that allow for RSDL in the first place. These exceptions are standard. But, as pointed out above, international law is clear that there are no circumstances or exceptions that permit for enforced disappearances, and yet creating exceptions is precisely what China has systematically done.

Because enforced disappearances undermine the deepest values of society, the widespread or systematic practice of enforced disappearances constitutes a crime against humanity. As noted in this chapter, while 'widespread' speaks to the large-scale nature of the act, 'systematic' is more about whether the act is part of a plan, practice, or policy. What matters is whether organization and predictability are present.

It should now be clear that RSDL is not simply a violation of China's obligations under international law, but that it is a systematic practice and policy achieved through a manipulated legal system; it embraces enforced disappearances as a tool of repression.

What's more, the experiences of those subjected to RSDL as presented in lucid first-person clarity through the stories in this book show that we can expect a degree of predictability to the abuse under RSDL.

Taken together, the preceding stories and legal analysis present a clear picture of China's systematic use of enforced disappearances. Should we consider RSDL as amounting to a crime against humanity? The answer to that is left to the reader.

Confronting China is no easy task but it is hoped that this book will serve as a wake up call to the extent of China's war on human rights.

END NOTES

Foreword | TENG BIAO

1 Inspired by the so-called Jasmine Revolution in Tunisia, and the broader Arab Spring movement, starting 20 February 2011, activists in China began calling for public assemblies in cities across the country to advocate for reform. After initially being met with overwhelming violence and repression, organizers started calling for people to assemble and "take strolls." Some 35 activists were detained, five of whom were charged with endangering state security. Many human rights defenders detained during this time, including Teng Biao, Tang Jitian, and Liu Shihui, were subjected to lengthy disappearances in which they were tortured. In many ways, the repressive extrajudicial tactics employed during this time can be seen as part of the inspiration for the current RSDL system.

2 Wang, Yaqiu. "What You Need to Know About China's 'Residential Surveillance at a Designated Place'." *China Change.* 2 August 2015. https://chinachange.org/2015/08/02/what-you-need-to-know-about-chinas-residential-surveillance-at-a-designated-place/.

3 Ibid.

4 Ibid.

5 The 709 Crackdown was a nationwide strike against both individual rights defense lawyers and the larger rights defense movement. Also known as the "war on lawyers." The name, 709, comes from the date when the first lawyer was detained, Wang Yu, on 9 July 2015. As part of the crackdown, over a period of months, some 300 lawyers were targeted, many of whom were placed in Residential Surveillance at a Designated Location. Some were sentenced to lengthy prison terms, such as rights defender Hu Shigen. In August 2016 he was given more than seven years in prison for subversion of state power; others were released following lengthy periods of incommunicado detention, torture, and forced confessions, such as lawyer Xie Yang. By many accounts, it has been the largest and most brutal crackdown on civil society since the 1989 Pro-Democracy Movement ended in the Tiananmen Square Massacre.

6 "Lǐ Wénzú: Zhōnggòng gōng'ān, huán wǒ zhàngfū Wáng Quánzhāng——Wáng Quánzhāng nǎ'er qùle?" 李文足：中共公安，还我丈夫王全璋——王全璋哪儿去了 (Li Wenzu: CCP Ministry of Public Security give my husband Wang Quanzhang back— Where is Wang Quanzhang?) *China Citizens Movement.* 16 May 2017. https://xgmyd.com/archives/29811.

Introduction | MICHAEL CASTER

1 Barefoot lawyers are unlicensed lawyers, human rights defenders who rely on the law in their rights defense. Sometimes called Citizen Lawyers or Cause Lawyers.

Because they lack a lawyer's license, these, often self-taught, lawyers work primarily with administrative law, such as filing lawsuits against government authorities for violations of rights, filing 'freedom of information' requests, handling appeals in land rights disputes and more. Due to the limited access to lawyers in China, for many outside the main cities, Barefoot Lawyers often stand as frontline legal defenders in the country.

[2] Rosenzweig, Joshua. "What Happens During 'Residential Surveillance?' *Siweiluozi's Blog*. 20 February 2012. http://www.siweiluozi.net/2012/02/what-happens-during-residential.html

[3] Bequelin, Nicholas. "Legalizing the Tools of Repression." *The New York Times*. 29 February 2012. http://www.nytimes.com/2012/03/01/opinion/legalizing-the-tools-of-repression.html

[4] Liu, Sida and Halliday, Terence C. *Criminal Defense in China: The Politics of Lawyers at Work*. Cambridge, Cambridge University Press: 2016. p.42.

[5] Following the abolition of the Custody and Repatriation System in 2003, local governments moved to establish ad-hoc underground prisons in provincial capitals and China's largest cities, to detain petitioners and forcibly send them back to their hometowns. The Black Jails varied in form ranging from massive prison facilities to a basement room in a back-alley hostel. The use of Black Jails reached its peak around the time of the 2008 Olympic Games. Following exposures in international media, coupled with domestic media interest, and the work of the Open Constitution Initiative, among others, to expose the system, its use has been reduced, but replaced with other secretive coercive measures.

[6] Wang, Yaqiu. "What You Need to Know About China's 'Residential Surveillance at a Designated Place'." *China Change*. 2 August 2015. https://chinachange.org/2015/08/02/what-you-need-to-know-about-chinas-residential-surveillance-at-a-designated-place/.

[7] Caster, Michael and Dahlin, Peter. "China Should be Proud of Wang Quanzhang, Instead it Persecutes Him." *The Guardian*. 23 September 2016. https://www.theguardian.com/world/commentisfree/2016/sep/23/china-should-be-proud-of-wang-quanzhang-instead-it-persecutes-him.

[8] Safeguard Defenders conversation with Chen Guiqiu.

[9] Lee Ming-che is a Taiwanese human rights defender and pro-democracy advocate affiliated with the Taiwan Association for Human Rights. His detention, forced confession, and trial garnered widespread attention and condemnation, amid widespread concern that his "confession" was forced under duress. In March 2017, Lee disappeared after entering China, from Macau, to meet with local human rights defenders. It was later revealed that the police had placed Lee under Residential Surveillance at a Designated Location before moving him to criminal detention and charged with threatening state security. He pleaded guilty at a trial in September 2017. His confession, almost certainly forced, was broadcast on Chinese state television.

[10] Lee Bo is a British citizen, and Hong Kong-based book publisher. Lee was one of five booksellers and publishers detained by China in what is known as the "Causeway Bay Book Disappearances." Lee disappeared in Hong Kong on 30 December 2015, last

seen at the time being pushed into a van by a group of men. Of the five men associated with the Causeway Bay Book Disappearances who were kidnapped and detained, Lee is the only one kidnapped in Hong Kong. Lee later showed up in detention in mainland China. He has remained mostly silent since his release, unlike fellow detained and kidnapped bookshop manager, Lam Wing-Kee.

[11] Safeguard Defenders conversation with Angela Gui.

[12] Lubman, Stanley. "China's Criminal Procedure Law: Good, Bad and Ugly," *The Wall Street Journal*. 21 March 2012. https://blogs.wsj.com/chinarealtime/2012/03/21/chinas-criminal-procedure-law-good-bad-and-ugly/.

[13] "We Can Dig a Pit and Bury you Alive: Annual Report on the Situation of Human Rights Defenders in China, 2011." Chinese Human Rights Defenders (CHRD). https://www.nchrd.org/wp-content/uploads/2012/03/We-can-dig-a-pit-and-bury-you-alive.pdf

[14] "Wave of Enforced Disappearances in China Sparks Concern from UN Rights Experts." *UN News Centre.* 8 April 2011. http://www.un.org/apps/news/story.asp?NewsID=38058#.WD6Y1yN962w.

[15] Email exchange between Michael Caster and human rights defender following the latter's release from secret detention.

[16] On 27 February 2017, Australia, Belgium, Canada, Czech Republic, Estonia, France, Germany, Japan, the United Kingdom, Sweden, and Switzerland issued a private letter to China's Minister of Public Security calling on the authorities to investigate allegations of torture against Xie Yang, Wang Quanzhang, and others and urging China to abandon its use of RSDL. However, the letter was issued privately and only later leaked to the press, leading some to question whether a more public criticism would have had more impact.

[17] "National Human Rights Action Plan of China (2016-2020)." *Xinhuanet.* 29 September 2016. http://news.xinhuanet.com/english/2016-09/29/c_135722183_6.htm.

Chapter 1 | TANG JITIAN

[1] Hua, Ze, Ed. *Mòlìhuā zài Zhōngguó: Zhènyā yǔ pòhài shílù.* 茉莉花在中国: 镇压与迫害实录. Taipei: Yunchen Wenhua. 2015.

Chapter 3 | WANG YU

[1] Cao Shunli was a human rights activist who died in a military hospital in 2014, amid allegations that she was denied essential medical treatment while she was in detention. Chinese authorities abducted Cao from Beijing Airport in 2013 as she was on her way to Geneva to attend a UN human rights review. Wang Yu was her lawyer.

[2] The Jiansanjiang incident of March 2014 involved several key rights defense lawyers in Jiansanjiang city, in northeastern China's Heilongjiang province. Lawyers Tang Jitian, Zhang Junjie, Wang Cheng, and Jiang Tianyong travelled to Jiansanjiang to investigate claims of torture of a group of Falun Gong practitioners being held in secret at a Black Jail. After visiting the site and returning to their hotel, Police

detained all four rights defenders and took them to the local police station, where they were severely beaten. News quickly spread through social media. Some human rights lawyers initiated hunger strikes to demand their immediate release, while others traveled to Jiansanjiang. Wang Quanzhang travelled to appeal for their release but was attacked in his hotel room, suffering broken bones and other injuries.

Chapter 9 | TANG ZHISHUN

[1] Tang, Zhishun. "Wǎngluò huàyǔ quán zhēngduó." 网络话语权争夺 (How to fight for the right of expression online). *草根之怒.* http://shamaonongmin.blogspot.com/2013/04/blog-post_15.html. 15 April 2013.

[2] Tang, Zhishun. "Kàng chāiqiān sānshíliù jì." 抗拆迁三十六计 (Thirty-six strategies for resisting illegal demolition). *草根之怒.* http://shamaonongmin.blogspot.com/2013/04/blog-post_14.html. 14 April 2013.

Chapter 10 | SUI MUQING

[1] An informal social movement taking its name from a May 2012 essay written by human rights lawyer Xu Zhiyong, the New Citizens Movement included many prominent figures such as Xu, Teng Biao, Li Fangping, Liu Ping, and others. Participants generally employed tactics of everyday resistance, and became well-known for hosting dinner parties, where small groups of rights defenders in different cities around the country would meet for clandestine talks and strategy meetings. The movement particularly focused on creating a culture of democracy and campaigned for more transparency and against corruption. Many of its members were arrested and sentenced to prison for their roles; Xu, for example, was sentenced to four years in prison in 2014.

[2] In January 2013, following the last minute removal of the New Year's editorial in the operationally more independent, although technically still state-owned, *Southern Weekly* newspaper in Guangzhou and its replacement with a flagrantly propagandizing editorial, journalists and rights defenders organized a series of demonstrations outside the newspaper headquarters. The demonstrations calling for greater freedom of expression lasted for over a week and generated considerable attention on Chinese social media and international coverage.

Chapter 11 | BAO LONGJUN

[1] See note 2 in Chapter 3 | WANG YU
[2] See note 1 in Chapter 3 | WANG YU
[3] Ilham Tohti is a moderate Uyghur scholar who was sentenced to life in prison in 2014 accused of separatism.
[4] Wu Gan is a human rights defender known for his colorful online activism under the pen name of Super Vulgar Butcher. He was swept up in the '709 Crackdown' and held for two years before being given a one-day, closed-door trial in August 2017 on charges of subversion. At the time of going to press, November 2017, no verdict had yet been made public.

In 2008, Wang Yu, then a commercial lawyer, got into a dispute with employees at a train station in Tianjin. After she filed a complaint, she was arrested for 'intentional assault' and sentenced to more than two years in jail. This injustice and her experiences of rights violations in jail inspired her to throw herself into rights defense work.

Chapter 12 | RSDL AND ENFORCED DISAPPEARANCES, A LEGAL VIEW

[1] *Enforced or Involuntary Disappearances*, Office of the United Nations High Commissioner for Human Rights. Fact Sheet No. 6/Rev.3, p. 1

[2] International Convention for the Protection of All Persons from Enforced Disappearance, Article 2.

[3] The three constituent elements of an enforced disappearance are enumerated in the Working Group on Enforced or Involuntary Disappearances "General Comments on the Declaration on the Protection of All Persons from Enforced Disappearances of 15 January 1996," and in subsequent expert opinions relating to the drafting of the Convention for the Protection of All Persons from Enforced Disappearance.

[4] *Report of the Working Group on Enforced or Involuntary Disappearance – Addendum: Best practices on enforced disappearances in domestic criminal legislation*, A/HRC/16/48/Add.3, 28 December 2010, para. 29.

[5] "General Comment on the definition of Enforced Disappearances", para. 7, in *Report of the Working Group on Enforced or Involuntary Disappearances*, A/HRC/7/2 2007, 10 January 2008.

[6] Working Group on Enforced or Involuntary Disappearances General Comment on Enforced Disappearance as a Continuous Crime.

[7] *Every minute counts – UN experts raise alarm over short-term enforced disappearances International Day of the Victims of Enforced Disappearances*. UNHCR. 30 August 2016. http://www.ohchr.org/EN/NewsEvents/Pages/DisplayNews.aspx?NewsID=20416

[8] *Report of the Working Group on Enforced or Involuntary Disappearances*, A/HRC/22/45, 28 January 2013.

[9] Working Group on Enforced or Involuntary Disappearances General Comment on the Right to the Truth in Relation to Enforced Disappearances.

[10] *General comment on women affected by enforced disappearances adopted by the Working Group on Enforced or Involuntary Disappearances at its ninety-eight session (31 October – 9 November 2012)*, A/HRC/WGEID/98/2. 14 February 2013.

[11] See: Declaration on the Right and Responsibility of Individuals, Groups and Organs of Society to Promote and Protect Universally Recognized Human Rights and Fundamental Freedoms, Adopted by General Assembly Resolution 53/144 of 9 December 1998; and Promotion of the Declaration on the Right and Responsibility of Individuals, Groups and Organs of Society to Promote and Protect Universally Recognized Human Rights and Fundamental Freedoms: protecting women human rights defenders, Resolution adopted by the General Assembly on 18 December 2013.

[12] *General Comment No. 31: The Nature of the General Legal Obligation Imposed on State Parties to the Covenant*.

[13] *Enforced Disappearances and Extrajudicial Execution: Investigation and Sanction*. The International Commission of Jurists. Practitioners Guide No. 9. 2015, p. 119.

[14] *Second Report on the Situation of Human Rights in Peru*, OAS/SER.L/V/II.106, Doc. 59 rev., 2 June 2000, para. 30. Cited in *Enforced Disappearances and Extrajudicial Execution: Investigation and Sanction.* The International Commission of Jurists. Practitioners Guide No. 9. 2015, p. 121.

[15] *General Comment on children and enforced disappearances, adopted by the Working Group on Enforced or Involuntary Disappearances at its 98th session (October 31 to November 9, 2012)*, A/HRC/WGEID/98/1 of 14 February 2013.

[16] International Convention for the Protection of All Persons from Enforced Disappearances, Article 6.

[17] Ibid., Article 4.

[18] Ibid., Article 7.

[19] *Enforced Disappearances and Extrajudicial Execution: Investigation and Sanction.* The International Commission of Jurists. Practitioners Guide No. 9. 2015, p. 169.

[20] General Comment No. 20 on article 7, Human Rights Committee or *United Nations Compilation of General Comments.*

[21] General Comment on women affected by enforced disappearances

[22] See: Basic Principles and Guidelines on the Right to a Remedy and Reparation for Victims of Gross Violations of International Human Rights Law and Serious Violations of International Humanitarian Law, adopted and proclaimed by General Assembly Resolution 60/147 of 16 December 2005.

[23] International Convention for the Protection of All Persons from Enforced Disappearance, Article 24(4).

[24] Basic Principles and Guidelines on the Right to a Remedy and Reparation for Victims of Gross Violations of International Human Rights Law and Serious Violations of International Humanitarian Law Adopted and proclaimed by General Assembly Resolution 60/147 of 16 December 2005, Article 19-23.

[25] Ibid., Article 24.

[26] See: Human Rights Council Resolution 9/11. Right to the truth, A/HRC/9/L.12.

[27] Report of the independent expert to update the set of principles to combat impunity, Diane Orentlicher, Addendum Updated Set of principles for the protection and promotion of human rights through action to combat impunity. E/CN.4/2005/102/Add.1 8 February 2005.

[28] International Convention for the Protection of All Persons from Enforced Disappearance, Article 24(2).

[29] Working Group on Enforced or Involuntary Disappearances General Comment on the Right to the Truth in Relation to Enforced Disappearances, para 1.

[30] Report of the independent expert to update the set of principles to combat impunity, Diane Orentlicher, Addendum Updated Set of principles for the protection and promotion of human rights through action to combat impunity. E/CN.4/2005/102/Add.1 8 February 2005.

[31] *General comment on women affected by enforced disappearances adopted by the Working Group on Enforced or Involuntary Disappearances at its 98th session (31 October – 9 November 2012)*, A/HRC/WGEID/98/2. Para 22.

[32] International Convention on Civil and Political Rights, 19(3)

[33] Working Group on Enforced or Involuntary Disappearances General Comment on the Right to the Truth in Relation to Enforced Disappearances

[34] Ibid.

[35] Human Rights Council Resolution 9/11. Right to the truth, A/HRC/9/L.12.

[36] Principle 2 of the *Set of Principles for The Protection And Promotion Of Human Rights Through Action To Combat Impunity* (E/CN.4/2005/102/Add.1)

[37] *Enforced or Involuntary Disappearances*, Office of the United Nations High Commissioner for Human Rights. Fact Sheet No. 6/Rev.3, p.3-4.

[38] *General comment on women affected by enforced disappearances adopted by the Working Group on Enforced or Involuntary Disappearances at its 98th session (31 October – 9 November 2012)*, A/HRC/WGEID/98/2. 14 February 2013. para 8.

[39] ICCPR (9(1)

[40] Communication No. 458/1991, *A. W. Mukong v. Cameroon* (Views adopted on 21 July 1994), UN doc. GAOR, A/49/40 (vol II), p. 181, para. 9.8.

[41] Ibid.

[42] ICCPR, Article 9.

[43] Communication No. 84/1981, *H. G. Dermit on behalf of G. I. and H. H. Dermit Barbato* (Views adopted on 21 October 1982), in UN doc. *GAOR*, A/38/40, para. 10 at p. 133.

[44] ICCPR 9

[45] Communication No. 336/1988, *N. Fillastre v. Bolivia* (Views adopted on 5 November 1991), in UN doc. GAOR, A/47/40, p. 306, para 6.5.

[46] ICCPR 14(3)(d)

[47] Body of Principles for the Protection of All Persons under Any Form of Detention or Imprisonment 18(3)

[48] Ibid.,15.

[49] International Convention on Civil and Political Rights, Article 14(3)(g)

[50] Declaration on the Protection of All Persons from Enforced Disappearance, Article 1(2).

[51] *Enforced Disappearances and Extrajudicial Execution: Investigation and Sanction.* The International Commission of Jurists. Practitioners Guide No. 9. 2015, p. 97.

[52] Ibid.

[53] Convention against Torture and other Cruel, Inhuman or Degrading Treatment or Punishment, Article 1(1).

[54] *Istanbul Protocol, Manual on the Effective Investigation and Documentation of Torture and Other Cruel, Inhuman or Degrading Treatment or Punishment.* Professional Training Series No. 8/Rev.1 United Nations, 2004. Para 10.

[55] *Enforced Disappearances and Extrajudicial Execution: Investigation and Sanction.* The International Commission of Jurists. Practitioners Guide No. 9. 2015, p. 99.

[56] Declaration on the Protection of All Persons from Enforced Disappearance.

[57] International Convention for the Protection of All Persons from Enforced Disappearance, Article 5.

[58] Rome Statute of the International Criminal Court, Article 7(1)(i) and 7(2)(a).

[59] *Enforced Disappearances and Extrajudicial Execution: Investigation and Sanction.* The International Commission of Jurists. Practitioners Guide No. 9. 2015, p. 100-101.

[60] International Convention for the Protection of All Persons from Enforced Disappearance, Article 1(2).

[1] Criminal Procedure Law of the People's Republic of China (2012). See China Law and Translate for English translation used here, Article 73.

[2] Ibid., Article 77.

[3] "China's New Criminal Procedure Law: "Disappearance Clauses" Revised," Dui Hua Human Rights Journal, 19 March 2012.

The People's Republic of the Disappeared

[4] Ibid.

[5] It is furthermore the obligation of the People's Procuratorate to inform the suspect of the right to a lawyer within three days of receiving the case for review toward prosecution and likewise the obligation of the Court within three days of receiving the case for trial. Criminal Procedure Law, Article 33.

[6] Criminal Procedure Law, Article 33.

[7] Ibid., Article 37.

[8] Ibid., Article 34.

[9] Ibid., Article 47.

[10] Provisions on People's Procuratorates' Oversight of Residential Surveillance in a Designated Location, Adopted 2015, Article 7(1) and 25.

[11] *Concluding observations of the fifth periodic report of China*, UN Doc. CAT/C/CHN/CO/5, 3 February 2016, para 14.

[12] Criminal Procedure Law, Article 73(1).

[13] Provisions on People's Procuratorates' Oversight of Residential Surveillance in a Designated Location, Article 4.

[14] Criminal Procedure Law, Article 73(1).

[1] Provisions on People's Procuratorates' Oversight of Residential Surveillance in a Designated Location, Article 9.

[2] Ibid., Article 17.

[3] Ibid., Article 19.

[4] Ibid., Article 16.

[5] Criminal Procedure Law, Article 37(3).

[6] Ibid., Article 83.

[7] Ibid.,Article 73(4).

[8] Provisions on People's Procuratorates' Oversight of Residential Surveillance in a Designated Location, Article 20.

[9] Ibid., Article 19.

[10] People's Police Law of the People's Republic of China, Article 44.

[11] National Security Law of the People's Republic of China (2015), Article 2 as translated by China Law Translate, http://www.chinalawtranslate.com/2015nsl/?lang=en, accessed on 9 November 2017.

[12] Article 105 reads, "Among those who organize, plot or carry out the scheme of subverting state power or overthrowing the socialist system, the ringleaders and the others who commit major crimes shall be sentenced to life imprisonment or fixed-term imprisonment of not less than 10 years; the ones who take an active part in it shall be sentenced to fixed-term imprisonment of not less than three years but not more than 10 years; and the other participants shall be sentenced to fixed-term imprisonment of not more than three years, criminal detention, public surveillance or deprivation of political rights. Whoever incites others by spreading rumors or slanders or any other means to subvert state power or overthrow the socialist system shall be sentenced to fixed-term imprisonment of not more than five years, criminal detention, public surveillance or deprivation of political rights; and the ringleaders and the others who commit major crimes shall be sentenced to fixed-term imprisonment of not less than five years."

[13] Regulations on the Procedures for the Handling of Criminal Cases by Public Security Organs (2015), Article 374.

[14] National Security Law, Article 7.

92077704R00137

Made in the USA
Middletown, DE
05 October 2018